Space

Terrace Books, a trade imprint of the University of Wisconsin Press, takes its name from the Memorial Union Terrace, located at the University of Wisconsin–Madison. Since its inception in 1907, the Wisconsin Union has provided a venue for students, faculty, staff, and alumni to debate art, music, politics, and the issues of the day. It is a place where theater, music, drama, literature, dance, outdoor activities, and major speakers are made available to the campus and the community. To learn more about the Union, visit www.union.wisc.edu.

Space

a memoir

Jesse Lee Kercheval

TERRACE BOOKS

A TRADE IMPRINT OF THE UNIVERSITY OF WISCONSIN PRESS

Terrace Books
A trade imprint of the University of Wisconsin Press
1930 Monroe Street, 3rd Floor
Madison, Wisconsin 53711-2059

uwpress.wisc.edu

3 Henrietta Street
London WC2E 8LU, England
eurospanbookstore.com

Printed in the United States of America

Library of Congress Cataloging-in-Publication Data

Kercheval, Jesse Lee.
Space : a memoir / Jesse Lee Kercheval.
pages   cm
ISBN 978-0-299-30024-1 (pbk. : alk. paper) — ISBN 978-0-299-30023-4 (e-book)
1. Kercheval, Jesse Lee—Childhood and youth.
2. Authors, American—20th century—Biography.
3. Florida—Social life and customs.
4. Outer space—Exploration.
5. Families—Florida. I. Title.
PS3561.E558Z47   2014
813'.54—dc23
[B]
2013043835

The author is grateful to the following persons and organizations for their support: the Graduate School of the University of Wisconsin, Ragdale, and the Wisconsin Arts Board. Special thanks to Gail Hochman, Shannon Ravenel, and my researcher, Dan Hughes Fuller.

Portions of this book in somewhat different form have appeared in these publications: *American Short Fiction, Calliope,* the *Colorado Review,* the *Missouri Review,* and the *Southern Humanities Review.*

My sister, me, and our mother, 1957

For Carol

Space

Prologue   Madison, Wisconsin, 1993

I open my front door and bend down to pick up the package the postman left. I'm bruised and sore from a car accident the week before, and so have to lift the box from the porch with my uninjured but awkward left hand. The box is full of family photographs I asked my sister Carol to send.

The night of the accident, I'd been driving home from a late meeting at the university where I teach, thinking perfectly ordinary, slightly harried thoughts, like, *Do I have enough detergent left to run a load of wash and if I don't what will my daughter and husband and I wear tomorrow?* The light was green at the last intersection before my house. I started across, was just shifting into third, when, out of the corner of my eye, I saw headlights. I've never been good at math, but my brain made this calculation with frightened speed: The headlights belonged to a car moving too fast to stop.

I'd been a passenger in a minor car accident a few years before and had ended up thoroughly black and blue. That was going to be nothing compared to this. A speeding car was about to slam into my driver's-side door. I remember thinking, *I'm dead.* Then, *Thank God, my daughter's not in the car.* And then, *I'll never write the memoir I was planning.* After that, I relaxed. It was out of my hands.

The car hit mine, and I went spinning across six lanes onto the other side of the highway. Luckily, my mental geometry had been off by a few feet. The other car had crushed the rear, unoccupied half of my car. I wasn't even bleeding. I had whiplash, a red stripe like a burn from the seat belt, and a cracked tooth where I'd hit my head on the side window. But I was miraculously, perfectly alive. Later, I would have to have a series of operations to try and fix my right hand, which had clutched the steering wheel in a brave but foolish attempt to save me.

I watched stunned as five teenage boys piled out of the other car. They were unharmed as well. Amazing. They, too, had been wearing their seat belts. The driver came over. He looked about twelve to me, with downy cheeks and soft puppy eyes. He was so sorry. He'd bent down to change the radio and hadn't seen the light turn red. He hadn't meant to be going so fast. It was his mom's car, he said. She was going to kill him. I managed to shake my head, the mother in me sure he was wrong. No matter what, she wouldn't prefer her son dead.

So life started up again. Except now I had no car. My family still had no clean clothes. But I would have time, with luck, to finish what I'd started.

Pictures seemed like a good place to begin, but I didn't have any. My sister, Carol, had kept them. The rationale behind this was that I moved around too much to haul family photos with everything else. And I *have* moved around too much. As I pick up the package of pictures that Carol has sent and feel how little it weighs, I realize how ridiculous this excuse is. The package is lighter than a book, and I've hefted boxes and boxes of books, apartment to house, town to city, state to state, for years.

The truth is that Carol kept the family pictures for the same reason—if you could call it by a name like *reason*—that she was the one in charge of keeping the family together all those years growing up. She thinks this has changed now that our parents are dead, that it is important that it change. In the matter of the pictures, at least, she is still the one in charge.

At first I just flip through the snapshots in my sister's shoe box to see what she has sent, what might be useful. I was afraid to be too specific about why I wanted the pictures. I wasn't sure how she would feel about my writing about our family. So she has sent an assortment, a grab bag of our life. The first one I pick up is a fuzzy, bluish color picture of me as a week-old baby. My head and hands show above a white blur of swaddling. I am lying in the middle of an equally white bed, and my mother's hands are just in the picture, resting on the mattress below my feet. I've seen the picture before, of course. I've even heard the story behind it. It was originally a slide and is in color (not black-and-white like all my later baby pictures) because one of the nurses at the hospital took the picture with her camera.

Looking closely, I can just see the gray metal railing at the edge of the bed. I was born in a hospital in France where my father was stationed as some sort of American liaison officer with NATO. I think I remember being told it wasn't an army hospital, but this looks like an army bed. My mother's hands, I would recognize anywhere. When I think of her, I think of her hands. In this picture they look large, competent, older than her age, which at the time was forty-one. Looking at them this time, they look subtly different to me. Now that I've seen my own hands next to a newborn baby daughter, I can imagine my mother felt less certain, less competent, than her hands look.

Sunlight falls in a slant across the bed, but is it early morning or late afternoon? My mother is wearing a watch, but it has turned on her wrist so I can't see the time. Right now that watch is somewhere in the bottom of my jewelry box, though it has a different band and the winding stem is missing. My mother wasn't a woman who wore much jewelry, and most of it is in this picture. On her left hand, she wears her engagement, a miniature version of my father's West Point class ring, and the matching wedding band. Carol has the engagement ring now, but on my left hand, the one that is holding the photograph, I wear the wedding ring. I had to have it cut down. My hands are smaller than my mother's.

I know I was delivered by cesarean section, as was my own daughter—lifted out of me; rescued from me, I sometimes joke—and that my mother and I were kept in the hospital for two long weeks. Still, where is my father? Why was the nurse the only one with a camera?

Now that I have a daughter, I respond to the baby in the picture more than I did before. If the infant me were here in the room, I would instantly pick her up. But the baby does not look like me. When I look at pictures of my daughter, I know her. When I first saw her in the operating room, it was as if I had already known her a long time. I thought, *Ah, there you are.* As if she had left the room for a moment, then stepped back in.

Did my mother feel that way when she saw me?

After a while, I put that picture down and pick up one of Carol and me. Then another. Always my sister's face is next to mine, the older sister bending over me. The photographs don't lie. She *was* always there, in the bath, the double bed, the backseat of the car. In these photos, taken with Brownies and Instamatics, our parents are only shadows, stretching dark along the foreground, or fuzzy index fingers wandering into the frame.

My sister's small face I'd know anywhere. I imagine my grown sister walking into the room right now, my smoothing her skin tight with my hands and finding that girl, the Carol in these pictures, hiding there. For myself, blond girl number two in these photographs, I still feel no recognition. I call the girl by my name, *Jesse*. But I have no sense that, yes, this is me.

I pick up a curling color print, KODAK KODAK KODAK printed in gray across the yellowing back, and flatten it with both hands. In it, Carol and the girl who must be me are standing in our backyard in Cocoa, Florida. Behind us, I can see the dark, glossy leaves of the orange grove next door. We both wear plaid shorts, white cotton shirts. Carol stands half a head taller. I am probably ten, Carol a wiser and older twelve.

In this picture, Carol and I seem to be holding shoe boxes

like the one in which my sister shipped these family memories to me, but actually they are elaborate cardboard viewers we have made following instructions printed in the newspaper. We are armed and ready to observe our first total eclipse. The sun is about to be blotted out by NASA's number one target, that object of all our desires, the moon. My sister and I are rooting for the moon, ready to see the home team win.

Before I had my daughter, before the accident, I used to think I had forgotten my childhood, had left it behind the way America built great rockets to reach the moon and then, losing interest, left the tons of metal to corrode in a swamp under a hot Florida sun.

I was wrong. The Florida of my past, where it is a humid, sunny ninety-five degrees, is always with me. At night, it makes me sweat just dreaming about it.

1 May 1966

We were supposed to stay at the Holiday Inn. But when my father asked the guy filling our gas tank at the Esso station off U.S. 1 where that might be, he just shrugged. There isn't one, he said. Not in Cocoa.

"This is Cocoa?" Carol said. I was nine, Carol eleven. Besides the service station, all we could see were four concrete lanes divided by a weedy median strip. I don't know what I'd expected—gantries with rocket ships lining the highways, astronauts in space suits riding motorized sidewalks? There weren't any sidewalks, moving or any other kind. The air conditioner in our Plymouth had frozen up, icicles dangled from the vents, but the rest of the car was unbelievably hot.

"Well," the attendant said, "there's more stuff down that way." He pointed south, the direction most of the traffic was headed.

We had driven three days from Oxon Hill, Maryland, a suburb of Washington, D.C., to get to Cocoa. My father had a job offer to be the business manager of the local junior college. He'd been teaching math, trying to put together a civilian life after thirty years in the army, and he was ready to move up. Still, on the trip down, he'd nodded in agreement whenever my mother said, Remember, we're just checking it out. She did not say so, but we all knew she hated the idea of leaving her job at the Treasury Department, where she was known for her ability to trace lost, forged, and stolen Social Security checks.

The president of the junior college was supposed to have gotten us rooms in the Holiday Inn. "Dr. Henry said he did, Mary," my father said to my mother. "I'm not making it up." It was nearly six. Too late, my father said, to call Dr. Henry. He was tense because we were lost and because he was driving. When my father drove, he gripped the wheel with both hands, like driving was hard work and needed constant attention. My mother drove with one hand resting lightly near the top of the steering wheel, a cigarette in the other. I liked to watch her. When she ran errands with Carol and me in the car, she sometimes told stories about being a WAC during the war, driving two-and-a-half-ton army transports on the busy Seattle docks.

A mile or so from the Esso station, my father pulled into the parking lot of a low, pale green building made of concrete blocks, not much more than a row of doors facing the highway: the Rocket Motel. At the edge of the parking lot, a rocket outlined in blue neon flickered in the sunlight over a hand-lettered sign: TV HOT WATER. The Rocket was not like any place we had ever stayed before. My parents were big fans of Holiday Inn, where the rooms looked just alike no matter where you were.

"Ask to look at the rooms first, Ed," my mother said as my father climbed out of the car, headed for the office. Carol and I scrambled out of the backseat. My mother had us dressed in matching plaid shorts and white blouses with Peter Pan collars. We were blond and had identical pixie haircuts. Once a day, at least, people asked if we were twins, something Carol hated but I didn't mind, since it meant I looked older than I really was.

The thing I hated was when someone mentioned my feet, which point out to either side like a duck's. If someone was a mom and being kind, she might ask if I took ballet. Kids, though, tended to stare and laugh. Carol's feet were perfect, her toes pointing straight ahead. She stood, rubbing the backs of her legs, which were red and lined from the car seat.

"Look," I said, pointing at the vacant lot beside the motel, "a palm tree." Carol looked. The palm was not waving gracefully like the coconut palms on *Gilligan's Island*. It was too short and stubby for that, its trunk armored with broken fronds. Still, it was a genuine outdoor palm tree, and I was excited. Carol shrugged. She wasn't.

"Come on," Carol said, pulling me toward the motel office. The tiny lobby was crowded with potted plants, like the ones our mother had back home but with thick, lushly tropical green leaves. Even living inside, they seemed to know they were in Florida. Philodendron covered the ceiling above the woman behind the counter. She was old and had grayish pink hair. My father was asking for two rooms. "There's only one left," she said. She spoke slowly, stretching out her vowels. "And I'm supposed to be holding it for this salesman. A regular customer."

My father shrugged, giving up. He was heading for the door when my mother came through it. Her hair was limp from the Florida humidity, and the gray in it was showing. If we'd been home in D.C., she would have been at the hairdresser. My mother was already fifty. She and my father hadn't married until she was nearly forty. When Carol and I were little and asked her how old she was, she told us thirtysix. It wasn't until we met her youngest brother, the baby of her family, and he said he was thirty-six that we found out she had lied to us. She laughed then and rolled her eyes, although I don't think she really thought it was funny.

"Please," my mother said to the woman with the gray-pink hair. She was sure now she wanted the room. "The girls are so tired." She waved a red fingernail at us. "It's been such a long day." My father had stopped just inside the door and was cleaning his glasses with his handkerchief.

"Your grandkids?" the woman asked.

My mother straightened. "My daughters." The woman looked from my mother to us and back again.

"Well," she said. "Joe'll kill me if he gets here and I've given away his room, but . . ." She paused. "I guess if he was coming, he'd be here by now." She handed my mother a white card to fill out. She printed *Col. and Mrs.* in front of our last name, though my father never used his rank anymore. The woman surrendered a key with a large green plastic tag.

I hung back when Carol and my father followed my mother out. I stood there kicking at the linoleum with one sneakered toe. I knew NASA was in the middle of the Gemini program, which was all about learning to do this and that—docking, walking in space. Things most kids I knew in D.C. found about as fascinating as watching the toddler down the block learn to tie his shoes. But after Gemini would be Apollo, and that meant the moon. I got up the nerve to speak. "Is there a space shot tonight?" I asked. The woman behind the counter smiled, shook her head.

"I don't think so, honey."

"Tomorrow?"

"It's not an airport," she said, losing patience with me, maybe with all Yankee tourists collectively. "Rockets don't go blasting off every hour."

OUR ROOM WAS tiny, nearly filled from light green wall to light green wall by two double beds. My mother pushed the button marked HIGH on the window air conditioner, and it came on with a whoosh and a groan. She stretched out on one of the beds. Above her on the wall was a faded color mural of three hoop-skirted Southern belles. One was sitting on a throne made of bright waxy oranges. The other two stood poised, as if ready for a game of musical chairs. I stood on the bed to get a closer look. In one corner it said *Citrus Queen and Her Court at World Famous Cypress Gardens*. I wondered if Cypress Gardens was in Cocoa and if we would get to go see it.

"Shoes," my mother said, pointing at mine. I flopped down next to her, dangling my offending sneakers carefully over the edge, but she had closed her eyes and wasn't watching. She had been this way the whole trip. Not like in D.C., where when she got home from work, she would fling open the backdoor and we would come running, Carol and I and our two dachshunds, Bertha and Gretel. Her two-legged girls and her four-legged girls, she called us. She came home full of stories, like the one about the two men named Apple who made the mistake of living on the same street, which, of course, thoroughly mixed up the delivery of their Social Security checks. She always gave Carol and me a Chiclet from her purse and asked how school was and what we wanted for dinner as she rubbed Bertha and Gretel on their long, wriggling stomachs. Already I missed the dogs. Locked in a kennel at the vet's along with our cat, Lucky, they probably felt the same way.

Carol filled one of the glasses in the bathroom with water. She took a taste. "Ugh," she said, "this is awful." My father took the glass from Carol, examined the yellow stain in the porcelain under the tap. He took a sip.

"Sulfur water," he said, swallowing. He made a point of taking another sip. "Not bad once you get used to it." My mother sighed and put her arm across her face.

"Well, I'm going to brush my teeth with Coca-Cola," Carol said.

It occurred to my father that we had not eaten. "I just can't get back in that car," my mother said.

"Maybe there's something we can walk to." My father opened the door of the room, letting in a damp wave of hot air, and looked out across the parking lot, across U.S. 1. "There's a shopping center across the highway. Surely there's something there."

"Take the girls," my mother said, her arm still over her eyes. I could tell she was hoping we would all go away.

"Aren't you hungry?"

"Bring me back something."

So it was my father who held our hands as we waited for a break in the traffic, which was mostly out-of-state cars like ours, but headed further south, to where there were probably real coconuts in the palm trees. My father held our hands as we walked, not ran, across the four concrete lanes. It was nearly seven o'clock, but it was as hot as ever, and the air was so humid it felt like you could grab a handful and wring it out like a wet sock. On the other side, we had to climb up a sandy bank and cross some railroad tracks to get to the shopping center. "Ouch!" Carol said. "Something stung me!" She pointed at the ground.

My father leaned down, examining the furry plant and its white flowers with some care. "It's a kind of nettle," he said at last. "Let's watch where we step."

So we watched. In spite of this, by the time we reached the shopping center's parking lot our socks were covered with little tan spurs. When we tried to pick them out, they stuck in the skin of our fingers. "Oh, well," my father said as he straightened, giving up on our socks. "Your mother will get them out."

He didn't offer to take our hands again, so we trailed

after him as he crossed the hot asphalt. The shopping center was green, too, like a bigger version of the motel. At one end was a department store, the name BELK'S spelled out above it in red neon, and, at the other end, Peebles Drugs. "I'll bet they have a lunch counter," my father said, basing this guess on some part of his life that predated us. No drugstore I had been in up to that point had ever had a lunch counter.

He was right. As soon as we stepped into the chill of the drugstore's air-conditioning, I smelled hamburger grease and cold bacon. We sat at the long counter that ran down one side of the store, and Carol and I took turns spinning each other on the high stools. My father didn't tell us to stop, though we all knew Mom would have.

Carol decided on a hot dog and a chocolate shake. To irritate her, I ordered the same. Dad ordered a BLT, asked for another BLT and a coffee to go, to take back to Mom. The waitress tried to pour him a cup, too, but he stopped her, his voice rising as he said, "No, thank you. I don't drink coffee." This was always happening. Usually he turned to my mother and said, I don't know why they think every man on the planet has to drink coffee. But since my mother was not there, he didn't. Carol got down off her stool. She was bored.

"What can I get you then?" the waitress asked.

"Just water," my father said, but then, remembering how the water here tasted, he changed his order to milk.

While the cook made the toast for the BLTs and the waitress spun the shakes around, Carol and I wandered through the store. The pharmacist in his white coat kept a careful eye on us from behind the prescription counter. The usual embarrassingly personal things were there, rubber mattress covers, pads for corns and even uglier body parts. But Carol found something good, a shelf of Florida souvenirs. I picked through the dusty display looking for something with Alan Shepard or John Glenn on it, but there was nothing like that.

It was all orange blossoms and flamingos and alligators. Carol settled on a jigger with a map of the state on it. At eleven, she already had an impressive jigger collection. I picked out a postcard with an alligator about to bite a woman in a bikini on the butt. Across the top it read *We Florida Alligators Would Rather Bite than Switch!* There were still cigarette commercials on TV then, and I thought the one about smokers who would rather fight than switch was funny, if not quite laugh-out-loud funny. By choosing something smaller and cheaper than Carol, I figured I was improving my chances of actually getting it. Carol frowned. She knew I was trying to make her look greedy.

We took our choices back to the counter with us. Dad had already finished half his sandwich, not calling or waiting for us, like he had forgotten we were with him. Our hot dogs were on the counter, but at first I thought the waitress had brought us someone else's order. Our mother always boiled hot dogs in the same small aluminum pot she used for soft-cooked eggs, and she served them in hot dog buns, but here the hot dogs were split in two and grilled and served between slices of toast with mustard and chopped onion. Florida-style, I guessed. Carol scraped the onions off hers with one finger, making a face. When we were finished, Carol showed Dad her souvenir jigger and asked him to get it for her.

"We're not in Florida on vacation," he said. "This is where we're going to live." Carol opened her mouth, and I knew she was thinking the same thing I was, that this was news to us and probably news to our mother. My father had only been pretending he hadn't made up his mind, that we would all get some kind of vote. I tried to imagine what living in Florida was going to be like, but all I had to go by was our room at the Rocket Motel. My father took the jigger from Carol, ready to pay for it, so she shut her mouth without saying anything. I gave him my postcard. Carol grinned at me. Her souvenir cost thirty-five cents, and mine only a nickel.

"Can I have a pack of gum, too?" I asked Dad when we were at the cash register. He had his wallet out, and he let the woman ring up the Juicy Fruit. He didn't even remind me to share it with Carol. She stuck her tongue out.

Outside, it was almost dark, but no cooler. While Dad went into the liquor store, Carol and I walked the length of the shopping center, past a shoe store, a card shop. We were all the way to Belk's by the time he came out. We heard him calling us. Carol held up one finger. One minute, she meant. She pulled open the glass door of the department store. A wave of refrigerated air hit us. The woman at the counter nearest the door looked up, startled. Or maybe it was only her painted-on eyebrows that made her look startled. Maybe she looked startled all day. She leaned over a regular forest of perfume testers. "Can I help you girls?" she said.

"No," Carol said, delighting in playing a small prank she knew we weren't going to be punished for, "you can't," and let the door fall shut again. We headed back toward Dad.

"She looked a little like Eve Arden," Carol said, and I knew she was baiting me. Eve Arden was a sore point with us. Carol insisted we used to watch *Our Miss Brooks* all the time, but I couldn't remember the show, so part of me suspected she was lying, that we had never watched it. If I said yes, the woman behind the cosmetics counter did look like Eve Arden, I'd be admitting we did watch it. If I said no, she didn't, I would be, too. Of course, probably we did watch it, only I had been too young to remember. If I said that, though, I would be admitting once and for all that Carol was not only older but wiser, and knew things I couldn't possibly know.

"She looked like Bozo the Clown is more like it," I said.

"Like Eve Arden playing Bozo," Carol said, not giving up.

Back at the Rocket Motel, Dad stopped by the office for a bucket of ice to go with the bottle of bourbon he had tucked under his arm. The bourbon was for my mother. She usually had a bourbon and water while she fixed dinner. My father rarely drank, and when he did, he drank Scotch.

We found Mom already in bed, smoking. She didn't touch the BLT or coffee. Carol and I got into the bathtub together, something we hadn't done in a long time, something we were really too big to do comfortably. The water bubbled around us and smelled terrible.

"God," we heard our mother say from the other room, "even the ice tastes like rotten eggs."

EARLY THE NEXT morning, my father went to the office to telephone Dr. Henry. When he came back he told us that though the college was in Cocoa, the Holiday Inn where we were supposed to be staying was on Cocoa Beach. "It's like this." He held out three fingers, touching the first. "This is Cocoa on the mainland," he said. He pointed to the space between his fingers: "Next comes the Indian River"—he moved to his second finger—"then something called Merritt Island"—he pointed to the space between his second and third fingers—"then the Banana River." Finally he touched his third finger. "Then Cocoa Beach. After that"—he waved his other hand at the limitless expanse beyond his fingers— "the Atlantic Ocean."

"Where's Cape Kennedy?" I asked.

My father pointed at his knuckles. "Here."

2

That first morning, we left the Rocket Motel and Cocoa and headed toward Cocoa Beach. In the years I lived there, I was to hear three different explanations of how Cocoa got its name, but I never found any of them particularly convincing. The most official was from the Federal Writers' Project guide to Florida, which said that Cocoa was named for the "Coco plum which grows abundantly there about." It sounds authoritative, coming as it does from the federal government, taker of censuses, maker of maps. Except no one I asked had ever heard of a coco plum. This was not an infallible test, since people who lived in Cocoa tended not to know much about Florida plants, so much like mad, giant houseplants, and so different from the Northern elms, hollies, and roses where they had grown up.

This was in spite of the education efforts of Cocoa's *Today* newspaper—*A Full Page of Color Comics Every Day!* —which ran recipes like PICKLED PALMETTO HEARTS. *Edible! Delicious! Dig them out of your own back yard!* As well as more cautionary tales, such as FAMILY OF FIVE DIES AFTER USING OLEANDER STICKS TO ROAST WEENIES.

It also seems unlikely that *coco plum* is a typo for *coco palm.* For though I have often seen the name of the town misspelled *Coco,* coconut palms do not grow as far north in Florida as Cocoa.

On this first trip to Florida, my dad's boss, Dr. Henry, had the privilege of being the first person to give me the most popular explanation of how the town got its name. He said the early settlers had been sitting around the general store trying to come up with a name when someone looked over and saw a tin of cocoa powder. "How about Cocoa?" that someone said. So they voted, and that was that. Cocoa carried the day.

This story is either too dumb or just dumb enough to be true.

The last explanation is really a variation on Dr. Henry's. In the old days, this one goes, when a steamboat went up and down the Indian River delivering supplies, the still-nameless settlement had been too new and too small to merit a stop. The inhabitants, made clever by necessity, nailed a cocoa tin on a piling in the middle of the channel so the boat could at least drop off their mail. The town became first *the Cocoa Drop,* then finally just *Cocoa.*

That no one knew which of these stories was true makes clear how profoundly it was a town, a whole people, whose time in this place went back no further than the Mercury program. First there was a swamp, then there were space-ships. Cocoa in 1966 was a place where history meant re-membering which of the practically new houses in our subdivision had been built first. It was a place on the map, an exit on the highway. And Cocoa Beach was *Cocoa, add water.*

To get to Cocoa Beach that first morning, we had to drive in our Plymouth across a causeway, over two tall-humped bridges above two shallow rivers, rivers so wide that, from the middle, the shoreline was only the faintest green smudge. My father repeated their names in turn: Indian. Ba-nana. Carol crouched on the floor of the car. The year be-fore, she'd decided she was afraid of bridges and announced this every time we drove over the South Capitol Street Bridge back in D.C.

However, these bridges were truly fearful. Each was so steep that my father unconsciously pulled back on the steer-ing wheel as if he were a pilot trying to get the nose of his plane up, so steep they seemed to end in midair. I had a hard time believing that when we reached the top we would not just sail off into space. I thought about how long it would take for the Plymouth to fall, whether it would be better to open the windows on the way down or after we hit the water.

As we reached the top of the second bridge and started down the far side, my father put the car into neutral, and we coasted like I did on my bike coming down a hill. Out the windows, all I could see was blue. Blue river, blue sky. My mother laughed for the first time on the trip. Below, a school of fish broke the surface, a fountain of silver splashes. Right behind them, a porpoise leapt into the air. "You're missing Flipper!" I said, kicking Carol. The porpoise nosed into the water, and the fish jumped again, higher, trying to escape being breakfast. Carol stayed on the floor, looking green.

On Cocoa Beach was another four-lane highway, this time lined by motels standing close together, as if these sandy lots were valuable in some way the sandy lots in Cocoa could never be. Fine sand blew across the highway, and the dividing line was so white in the sunlight it hurt my eyes. Even my parents, who were both wearing dark green prescription sunglasses, squinted.

The Holiday Inn looked just like a Holiday Inn, and our rooms just like Holiday Inn rooms. A band of paper stretched across the toilet seat to guarantee it had been sanitized, and each drinking glass was wrapped in white, waxy paper. My mother took off her sunglasses and nodded her approval, obviously relieved, though the water still tasted funny. We went for breakfast and ordered off the standard Holiday Inn menu. During the two breakfast stops on the way down, I had tried to order Our Special Strawberry Waffle. At each stop, the waitresses said they were out.

In Cocoa Beach, I asked and received. My father smiled at the waitress, told the story. "Would you believe this is the third Holiday Inn . . ." The waitress smiled.

"Do tell," she said.

"Jesse's our waffle girl," my mother said. I nodded to acknowledge the compliment—*that's me all right*. I was always asking her to fix waffles for dinner, something she did now and then. I did this so I could follow my father's lead and have first a waffle with a fried egg and bacon and then another with strawberries—for dessert. I liked waffles for dinner because it seemed weird to be eating breakfast at five o'clock at night, to stand a day on its head like that. I liked the idea, but I was not really sure I liked waffles, which, at least as my mother made them, were always a bit heavy.

Only when the waffle arrived, as big as my head and festooned with frozen strawberries and canned whipped cream, did I remember this. Carol looked at me and shrugged. I ate bravely away, and in a little while Carol and my father helped me. It wasn't important that I, or even we, finish the waffle. We weren't a clean plate family. Commenting on what anyone ate or didn't eat seemed a bit too personal. I just needed to look like I enjoyed it so it would make a good ending to the story of how I searched and searched until finally, in the place we were soon to call our home, I found my strawberry waffle.

By the time the waitress came back for our plates, the waffle had been sufficiently mauled.

I cleared my throat. "I don't suppose," I said, being more cautious, more adult in my approach this time, "there's going to be a shot anytime soon? I suppose if there were, Walter Cronkite would be here." The waitress leaned close, rested one hand on the back of my chair.

"Not always, Sweetie," she said. "Sometimes, with no notice at all, they send up one of these secret spy satellites. Your boyfriend or your daddy gets called into work one Sunday and the next thing you know, the plates are rattling in the cupboards, and there one goes." The waitress straightened, refilled my mother's coffee. "They're kind of puny, though, as rockets go."

AFTER BREAKFAST, WE went to look at houses. Just to see what was available, our father said. He drove us to a neighborhood on Cocoa Beach that Dr. Henry had suggested. The houses were stucco, painted different dreamy pastels: aqua, pink, turquoise—colors I had never seen a house painted. Our house back home was red brick with black wood shutters, as were all the houses in our neighborhood, in all the suburbs that sprawled into Maryland and Virginia from D.C. On the wall by the front door of each Florida pastel house was a starfish or conch shell molded out of white cement. The lawns were bright green, with sprinklers sweeping back and forth across them. Rainbows hovered above the arcs of water. "Phew, smell that sulfur," my mother said.

A Realtor, a fiercely tanned woman with dark cat's-eye sunglasses, met us at the model house, a pale yellow one with a sea horse by the door. Carol and I raced through the rooms. "Hey, our bathroom has two sinks," she called. "No more sharing." The walls inside were stucco, too, and felt rough when I brushed against one. A glint of light caught my eye, and I looked up.

"Wow, look," I said to Carol. The stuccoed ceiling glittered as if stars were mixed with the plaster, or at least bits of mica. Carol wrinkled her nose.

"Tacky," she said.

The floors were something the Realtor called terrazzo. It looked like marble, with chips of gold and silver dreaming away below the polished surface. It reminded me of a story a girl at school told, about how her goldfish got caught by a freeze in their pond and stayed that way all winter and then thawed out in the spring, good as new.

I ran through the open sliding-glass door into the back-yard. Here the lawn sloped down to a canal about as wide as the driveway. A powerboat went by, and a brown wake washed the edge of the grass. Across the canal, at what could be our neighbors', a sailboat was tied to a dock. The sound of the rope clanging against the mast was exactly the same sound the flagpole had made all year outside my fourth-grade classroom. I wondered if our dogs would like it here. I wondered if dachshunds could swim. Our cat, Lucky, wouldn't be keen about being surrounded by so much water. The Realtor came out with my parents.

"It's awfully small," my mother was saying. She was think-ing of our house in Maryland, which was two stories and had a full basement.

"That's because you're from up North," the woman said, taking her sunglasses off long enough to wipe them with a tissue. She had white ovals around her eyes. "Everyone thinks that about Florida houses at first. You have to realize, here you do most of your living outside." My mother pushed her own sunglasses up with one finger. She looked doubtful. It wasn't even noon, and already the sun was so hot that the canal was steaming. My father took the Realtor's card.

On the way back to the Holiday Inn, my father talked

about getting a paper, calling another Realtor or two. "Let's sleep on it, Ed," my mother said. So instead, we went to the beach.

I had never been to a beach before, but I had grown up seeing all the world's oceans on TV and in *National Geographic*. I thought I knew what the Atlantic would be like. Then I walked with Carol out the rear door of the Holiday Inn, crossed the hot wooden boardwalk hopping on one foot, and as far as I could see there was only hard tan sand and ocean. Water stretched to the horizon and out of sight on either side, too. For the first time, I knew the meaning of the word *endless*. The waves were different than I thought they would be. I imagined splashes, like in a pool. Long swells started at the edge of the horizon and rolled toward me like moving hills. I couldn't take my eyes off them.

"Cowabunga," Carol said, quoting Snoopy, and ran for the water.

I followed her, stood an inch in the surf. I felt dizzy with the idea that each wave had started in England or in France where I was born or in whatever place was on the other side of all that long, lonely ocean and had come all this way to end here, breaking into white foam on my toes.

My father rented an already inflated inflatable raft from a stand on the beach and took us out. Carol and I couldn't really swim. We had just dog-paddled a little in the swimming pool at the officer's club my father still belonged to outside D.C. It was always so full of people you could walk across it without getting wet. Our skills weren't up to an ocean. My father's barely were. He had been on the swim team when he was at West Point, and my mother complained that when he was restless at night he still swam in his sleep, but I had never seen him do more than a couple of slow laps.

My mother stayed on the beach, fully dressed, a towel draped over her head. She never went in the water. She waved. Carol and I clung to the raft as my father sidestroked into the waves, dragging us along on our raft with one hand. A wave crested right in front of us, slapped us full in the face. I heard Carol shriek, but I was too amazed.

The water was really salty. I mean, I knew the water in the ocean was saltwater, but I had thought of it as something very dilute, like the few grains of sugar my mother put in her coffee. This stung my eyes and made the inside of my nose burn like crazy. I licked my lips. It was like licking a potato chip, that salty. "Hang on," my father said, stroking away. Another wave got us, and Carol gave up, went splashing back to the beach to join my mother under her towel. She should have stayed. Dad towed me out beyond the surf, and we floated there, rising and falling on the swells.

"This is the life, eh?" he said, floating on his back, wiggling his toes. He was still wearing his prescription sunglasses. Back home, he never went in the pool without them. After a while, we saw my mother standing up. She waved her arm back and forth over her head. We both understood perfectly that she wanted us to come in and get out of the water, but we didn't. For a good long while, we ignored her, like we were both adults and knew better. Then Carol began hopping around, too. "They'll spook the lifeguard," Dad said, angry. We ignored them a second longer, then my father sighed, resigned. "We'd better head in."

We were about halfway when a wave caught him from the side and swept his sunglasses off. "Goddamn it, those cost me thirty bucks," he said, letting go of the raft and diving for them.

The next wave took hold of the raft and spun me forward, high on the crest. I hung on, surfing along. Then the curl caught the nose of the raft and pulled it under and me with it. Suddenly I was on the bottom. I felt coarse sand, broken shells. I heard the strange underwater sound of my skin scraping along the ocean floor. I tried kicking my legs, but my muscles were nothing compared to the pull of the undertow, sucking me out to sea with the other trash.

In a moment, I knew, I would be drowning. In front of my eyes I saw a newspaper with the front-page headline NONSWIMMER DROWNS. Below that, a picture of what was left of my family: Mom, Dad, Carol. I felt cheated. I was supposed to see my whole life flash in front of my eyes. Everyone knew that. Could it be that at nine I hadn't had enough of one yet?

Then it was over. The surge of the next wave pulled me up out of the undertow, spun me over and over until I found myself sitting in about a foot of water. I stood up. My bathing suit bottom was full of wet, heavy sand. "Oh, there you are," my father said. He had his sunglasses in his hand.

AT DINNER, THE waitress looked at me, took a step back, and said, "Boy, did you get some sun!" She looked from me to Carol, who was white as wax by comparison.

My mother pressed her finger to my nose. "Good Lord," she said, "you're blistered."

Tucked into bed coated with Noxema, I felt the surf rising and falling, as if the bed were the raft and sleep another ocean. My mother's voice drifted in from the next room. "Well, all right," she was saying, "but you'll have to break the news to the girls. They don't seem so crazy about Florida."

"Jesse is," my father said. "I can tell."

Lying there, close to sleep, even I wasn't sure which parent was right, which one wrong.

That night, it turned out, Carol and I had the same dream.

Except hers was more like a nightmare. We both dreamed that we were with our parents, driving over the causeway to Cocoa Beach, but this time when we reached the top, the other half of the bridge really wasn't there. In my dream, we hit the water, but we didn't sink. The tires caught hold, and we drove down the river as if the Plymouth were a power-boat. We cruised into a canal and pulled up at the dock of our new yellow house.

In Carol's dream, the car sank under the water, down so deep in the mud at the bottom that we couldn't get the doors open or roll down the windows. We didn't drown though. We were just stuck there, like we were on a family vacation somewhere where there was nothing to see, and we were taking forever to get there.

THE NEXT NIGHT we went to Dr. Henry's house for dinner to celebrate my father's accepting his new job. It turned out they lived in the neighborhood where we had seen the yellow model house. We even passed it, sprinklers spinning in the twilight. Even though I pointed, my parents didn't so much as glance at it. Wherever we were going to live, I had the feeling it wasn't going to look like that. The Henrys' house was turquoise with a white porpoise by the front door. Mrs. Henry let us in. She had silvery blond hair and wore a short white skirt like she was about to or had just played some tennis. Even compared to the other Floridians we had seen, she was incredibly tanned. She kissed first my mother, then Carol, then me. She took my father's hand. Her silver bracelets slid together with a delicate click.

"We're so happy to have you here," she said. She had a slight Southern accent.

"We're just so happy to be here," my father answered her, with a pretty thick fake one. Mrs. Henry laughed.

My mother was wearing a gray knit suit with a scalloped neckline, the kind of thing she would have worn at work for an especially important meeting. Even then, she had trouble with her feet, and so had on black lace-up shoes. She looked like Mrs. Henry's mother, and maybe she was old enough for that to be possible. She had dressed Carol and me for the occasion in the usual white blouses and matching plaid, except that we were wearing skirts this time instead of shorts.

"Don't you girls look nice," Mrs. Henry said, smiling first at Carol, then me. Carol frowned, so I answered.

"Thank you, Mrs. Henry."

"Lucille," she said. "*Everybody* calls me Lucille."

Dr. Henry was dressed in white, too, a short-sleeved shirt open at the neck. He had brown hair and soft brown eyes, a long nose. He looked awfully young to be my father's boss. He also looked a lot like the half-grown puppy that followed him to the door, a beagle introduced as Max. My father relaxed when he saw Dr. Henry's shirt was unbuttoned. My mother had wanted him to wear a tie, but my father had decided against it. No one in Florida wears one, he'd said. It seemed that he was right.

"So who wants a drink?" Dr. Henry asked my father as soon as we were inside. He had fixed a frozen drink—he called it a daiquiri—and poured one for my father. He filled another glass from the blender, held it up. "You, Mary?" Dr. Henry asked. My mother, as a bourbon drinker, had a low opinion of sweet mixed drinks, but she nodded and took the glass from Dr. Henry. My father smiled at her, happy she was trying.

Mrs. Henry appeared with some Hawaiian Punch for Carol and me. She had put orange slices in the glasses and added little paper parasols. Carol rolled her eyes. *Tacky.* I ignored Carol, smiled, and said, "Hawaiian Punch is my favorite. Thanks so much, Mrs. Henry." Mrs. Henry laughed a wonderful hoarse laugh and clinked her bracelets.

"Lucille," she said, touching me lightly on the head. She was smoking now, not Winstons like my mother smoked but some brand that smelled pleasantly mentholated, like Noxema. She put a parasol in my father's glass and said something I didn't catch. My father laughed. He was having a good time, and it occurred to me that he was flattered by Mrs. Henry's attention, that we both were.

Mrs. Henry clapped her hands. "We're having red snapper," she announced. "I hope everyone likes it." There was a slight silence, and I suspected I was not the only one in the room who had no idea what a snapper was.

"Fish is fine," my mother said, and she was right, fish it was. Fresh, with an eye and a tail and everything.

Mrs. Henry served our plates. Carol did not say *gross,* but I could hear her thinking it. "This much?" Mrs. Henry asked me, holding up an adult-size serving. I nodded, taking the portion as a sign of respect.

At home we had fish sticks sometimes or frozen sole. It was not my favorite food but fell under the general heading of *not bad.* I took a bite of the snapper. I blinked. Red snapper was simply the best nondessert thing I had ever tasted in my life, a food beyond my experience with food. It was not fishy and was so light that by comparison every meat I'd known before was as heavy and greasy as pot roast. I swallowed.

Mrs. Henry was watching me. She raised her neat blond eyebrows. *So?*

"It's wonderful," I said. "Really wonderful. I love it." Carol shot me a look, but for once she was in no position to tell me *like* was the right word, that you cannot love things that can't love you back. I did love it. Loved the idea of a world full of fruits and vegetables and fish I didn't know existed, didn't even have names for. I couldn't wait to live in Florida, to eat a new food a day.

"It's wonderful, Lucille," my father said. "You'll have to give Mary the recipe."

"It's so simple," Mrs. Henry said, laying two tanned fingers on my mother's wrist. "But you have to get a really fresh fish."

"I imagine so," my mother said.

After dinner, Dr. Henry volunteered to make the coffee. He and my father, the man who never drank coffee, went into the kitchen to consult on this. My mother shook her head. For the first time all evening, she and Mrs. Henry were in on a joke together, and the joke was men. My mother lit first her own, then Mrs. Henry's cigarette.

Mom stood looking at Mrs. Henry's white bamboo living-room set. "Maybe I shouldn't bother to move my old furniture down. It's all cherry," my mother said, softly. "So dark." She inhaled deeply and then let the smoke trickle out through her nose, as if this were serious and she was asking Mrs. Henry for her best advice.

"It's so hard to know what . . ." Mrs. Henry started to say.

Max interrupted. He was standing with his front legs up on the back door, barking to go out. To me, he looked tall for a beagle, but then all dogs look tall after you've been around dachshunds. "Excuse me a minute, Mary," Mrs. Henry said to my mother. She flipped a switch and outside floodlights came on. "Keep me company?" Mrs. Henry asked me as she opened the sliding-glass door. I nodded. Carol, standing close to our mother, frowned at me as if my acceptance were some kind of betrayal. I followed Mrs. Henry out.

Where the model house had a backyard, the Henrys' had a pool. The turquoise water glowed in the humid night. Max ran out of the light into the night. "Max!" I called and started after him.

"Don't worry," Mrs. Henry said. "The yard's fenced. Has to be for the pool." She stood next to me, smoking. We listened to Max moving somewhere in the darkness, to the whine of mosquitoes hovering inches from our ears. Mrs. Henry let out a long sigh of menthol smoke, and the mosquitoes retreated. It was really quite a big pool, almost as big as the one at the officer's club at home, or rather, I corrected myself, back in Maryland where we used to live. At the far end was a pile of life jackets and Styrofoam floats.

"I teach swimming here in the summer," Mrs. Henry said. "Do you know how to swim?" I thought about how I had almost drowned, about the rough ocean floor, and it seemed strange to be here, breathing.

"No," I said. "Not really."

"It's a waste to live in Florida and not swim," she said. "Would you like to take lessons?"

Lessons. Of course, I thought, standing in the hot, thick night. To live in Florida, you needed lessons. I nodded.

"Good," Mrs. Henry said. She leaned down and kissed the top of my head, breathing smoke into my hair like a warm and mentholated blessing.

3

There are parts of a person that can never be in a photograph. A picture cannot catch the way someone moves or sounds. When people did something odd, my mother was apt to say, To each his own, said the old lady as she kissed the cow. When faced with some sign of trouble, she'd sigh, shake her head, and say, We're only born to suffer and die. Strange as it sounds, this always cheered her up. After all, if we are only born to suffer and die, by comparison this day's trials are minor league. My mother didn't go to church, but the Calvinism of her ancestors was in her bones like damp. She had a strong sense of impending doom, and though I don't believe we are sinners in the hands of an angry God, I find I do, too.

Not all of her sayings were quite so dire. When confronted with Jell-O, she would make a face and say, You put it in your mouth, and then what do you do? When she cooked dinner, she sometimes sang a song whose refrain was "I didn't know the gun was loaded, and I'll never ever do it again."

The saying of hers that ruled our lives more than any other was: Don't talk about people, talk about things. Compared to her comments on the consistency of Jell-O, it is not a particularly pithy saying. After years of teaching English, I can't read the word *things* without wanting to circle it in red and write *Inherently Vague* in the margin. But I knew then and know now what she meant.

She meant she wasn't interested in gossip, that it was better to take the long view, to talk about history, about the events on the evening news that would be history, to start every sentence with a polite "Did you see the article in *Time* about . . ." She meant if you had to talk about what was important in your own life, talk about it as if it were already history, with a certain dry and dispassionate distance. Events of the day were interesting or instructive, never heartbreaking or joyous or unbearable.

She meant that you should keep some distance from life, particularly your own life, that the world was divided into public and private spheres, and even our own dinner table was public. An Irish Catholic friend who taught for a while in Utah once told me that when, in the course of lecturing on *Hamlet* or *Moby Dick,* she wandered into some territory her Mormon students found offensive, they would simply look at the ceiling until she gave up and moved on to something else. Only then would they bring their eyes down to meet hers and warm her with their smiles.

My mother did the same thing. If I started into some confession, some betrayal of emotion that struck her as altogether too personal, I knew it without her saying a word. Her smile would shut off as if she had suddenly left her body, the table, me. I imagined her floating near the ceiling, fingers in her spirit ears, humming *The Stars and Stripes Forever* to keep from hearing a word I said. Only when I stopped, my story dying away without a middle or an end, would she drift down and rejoin her still-seated body, smile, and ask me what I wanted for dessert.

The lesson was clear. If even our dinner table was public, only your own head was really private. I will never know how much she knew of what went on in mine. I can only guess what went on in hers.

One of the pictures my sister has sent me is of my mother with me, as a baby, in her lap. If I am that little, we must still be in France, and so the overstuffed chair we sit in, though it appears ordinary in every way, must be a French chair. Carol is there, too, of course. Leaning forward, one eye on the camera, about to plant a dramatic kiss on her baby sister's cheek. My mother is smiling, the warm, slight smile that was her best reward, but at something outside the square boundaries of the photograph: a window or mirror or maybe something boiling on the stove.

I am too young to be talking in the picture, saying something my mother doesn't want to hear. Still she looks somewhere else, smiling vaguely, as if she weren't quite there, as if there were other places she would rather be. When I play with my own daughter, I sometimes find myself drifting, too, looking at the TV or a magazine out of the corner of one eye. I smile and say, Back in just a minute, have to check the stove. I use any old excuse to get up off the floor and go.

But where? Once in the kitchen, I find myself just standing, staring out the door. So I need to know what my mother was waiting and watching for. A different life and the moving van to take her there? I imagine she was waiting even as a child, looking out a window for a sign of rescue, some small bird, a hidden angel, to stop and pull the sadness from her like an earthworm pulled from good ground.

She was waiting from the moment she was born, in Morehead, Kentucky, now home to a fair-size college with a decent basketball team, but then just a small coal town in the Appalachian Mountains. Her father, J.L., was a contractor during the Depression, when no one was building much of anything. After the war, he bought a coal mine just in time to see the bottom drop out of that market as well. My mother was born on either April 25 or 26, 1917. The family disagreed about the actual date, so she liked to claim both days. Why not? She didn't use the two days to double her celebration as much as to deny either of them the power of making her another year older.

I have no proof she was born with that slightly distant air she has in my baby picture. No pictures of my mother as a baby are in the shoe box my sister has sent. They were all lost along with my grandparents' house in the Great Morehead Flood of 1939. On the Fourth of July, with no warning, water swept through the town, washing my grandparents' house off its foundation, sweeping all their belongings away. My mother said she had to spend the night in a tree, clinging to her younger brother, who had a broken leg.

When the water went down, they found their grandmother dead in the house, stuck head down in the mud that had filled the kitchen. As a young girl, my mother had been sent for a while to live with her grandmother and take care of her. She was bitter about this, and she always seemed to say "stuck head down in the mud" with a certain grim satisfaction. After all, we are only born to suffer and die.

The earliest surviving picture of my mother is one taken when she was four or five. She is sitting on a lawn with her only sister, Ellie. Ellie was two years older. Carol is two years older than me. Ellie and my mother are wearing matching white dresses and holding brand-new dolls. The dolls have Kewpie doll faces and bee-stung lips like flappers, but their hair is in long braids and they each wear a headband with a single fluffy feather stuck in it. They are Indian maidens.

Ellie is looking right at the camera. Her dark hair gleams, her dark eyes as well. She smiles as if she had a secret she would just love to whisper in your ear. Ellie was the pretty one, my mother always said. My mother once overheard a great aunt say that it was shame Ellie didn't have my mother's good skin, that it was wasted on a plain girl like her. In this picture, my mother is squinting as if the sun were too bright, though my aunt's eyes are wide open. For once, Mother is looking in the general direction of the camera. Here, it is her doll whose coy eyes gaze sideways at something or someone beyond the frame.

My mother's family always called her by her full name, *Mary Olive*. Ellie was always *Ellie Mae*. They had the Southern habit of double names, but my mother never liked the *Olive* part. She was tall and thin and altogether too like Popeye's Olive Oyl to avoid being teased. She graduated from high school in a class of eight and went on to get a B.A. in home economics at the teacher's college in her hometown. She said it was the only science degree women were allowed to take.

In the shoe box I find a tiny, square black-and-white snapshot I have never seen before. My mother is in some sort of test kitchen with one other girl, who is dropping cookie dough onto a baking sheet and smiling at the camera. Mother stands at a big white stove wearing a stiff, striped apron and does not look at the camera or smile. She appears to be waiting for the largest tea kettle I have ever seen to boil. She has exactly that distant look I recognized in my baby picture. It is as if the kettle were more than a kettle, and she is waiting, watching, and listening for something more than the white hiss of steam.

Having a degree in the science of being a homemaker didn't make my mother want to be one. She was an awful cook. She tended to read a recipe and remove what she felt were unnecessary ingredients, until stew became *boil one pound meat in one gallon water until both are gray*. When Lipton's Onion Soup Mix came on the market, she started adding that to everything, stew, pot roast, meat loaf. It was a real improvement.

My mother acted as if taste in food was dangerous. If called upon to make something special, she fell back on eye appeal, following the lead of the color pictures in her *Family Circle* or *Betty Crocker* cookbooks. She would drape canned asparagus over lettuce wedges or arrange canned pears on lettuce leaves and decorate them with a dollop of mayonnaise and a sprinkle of cheddar cheese. In general, she cooked as if she resented it as much as she resented not having been allowed to study something more worthwhile. She would have liked to have been a doctor, she once told me. But it wasn't possible.

She graduated from high school when she was seventeen. Then she taught school, up in the mountains where many of her students were older than she was. So far back in the hills the sun don't shine, she used to say. Where her students' mothers sewed them into their long underwear for the winter, and they didn't bathe from fall until spring. It took her eight years to finish her B.A., teaching all the while. So she jumped at the chance to get away, and her chance was the Women's Army Corps. In 1942 when she enlisted, the idea of women in the army was controversial, and the government was very cautious. Recruits had to be college graduates whose backgrounds had been thoroughly checked by the FBI.

My mother made it in and left Kentucky and her family behind. She also left half her name. In the WACs, there were so many Marys they used middle initials to keep them straight. My mother became *Mary O.*, and she never used *Olive* again. When I was pregnant with my daughter, my husband and I had a hard time agreeing on possible baby names. I vetoed all his family names, he returned the favor. Finally he suggested Olivia, in honor of my mother. I told my sister. "Mom would spin in her grave," she said. She was right. In the end, we picked a name no one we knew had ever had.

My mother said she discovered the world in the WACs. She was posted to Toledo, Ohio, where she had pizza for the first time and danced the polka at somebody's wedding. Then she went to sea, sailing back and forth across the treacherous North Atlantic evacuating wounded soldiers. She rose to the rank of major, a very high rank for a woman in those days.

There are more pictures of my mother in the service than of anything else in the box. Marching in long lines of women. On a bus with nothing but men. There are several snapshots that seem to have been taken at parties or in officers' clubs. Men in uniforms, women in suits with white corsages on their lapels. In these, she is smiling directly at the camera as if she were happy for the first and maybe only time in her life. In one, she hugs a pillar in the middle of a dance floor, her head thrown back. She is obviously laughing and maybe a bit drunk.

Then in 1953 she left the WACs and married my father, demoted from major to army wife. In those days, she told me, you couldn't be married or have children and also be a WAC. She gave birth to my sister, followed my father when he was ordered to France, discovered she was pregnant again, and had me. I can tell all that from the outside, from the record, from the pictures. But what happened to her really? All I know is she changed names again. My father called her just *Mary,* or, more often, *your mother.* As in, I don't know, ask your mother, or, Tell your mother where you'll be.

The last photograph in the box is a color snapshot of my mother sitting at the kitchen table in our house in Cocoa. I took this one with my first camera, an Instamatic. I'd asked for one for Christmas so I could take pictures of my friends. By this time, for reasons I didn't understand and no one seemed willing to explain to me, Mother was spending most of each day in bed. I wanted to try out my new camera, so I snuck up on her as she was having her morning cup of instant coffee. Just before I pushed the button, she saw me.

"Oh, no," she said, and raised her hand to cover her face. So there she is, a woman with gray hair that needs a new permanent, frozen in her bathrobe in that unhappy moment as my mother. Not looking at the camera or away from it, not looking anywhere at all, as if she had nowhere she wanted to look, nothing she wanted to see anymore. Behind the blur of her hand hiding her face, I can see her eyes are closed, too, as if her life were a double-locked door.

4   June 1966

My father called to say he'd found a house. My mother, Carol, and I had flown back to D.C. so Carol and I could finish the last three weeks of school and my mother could sell our old house; he'd stayed behind and started work in Florida. We all took turns asking, but my father refused to describe the new house. We'd see it soon enough, he said. The family living in it would be moving as soon as school was out. My mother already had an offer for our house from a family who would be moving from California as soon as school ended there. I had a vision of families all over the country moving at the end of the school year, like one giant Chinese fire drill. I couldn't wait.

I couldn't make myself pay attention in school. We were studying Maryland history in fourth grade. What was the point? I was already a Floridian, and in Florida there would be different names and dates to learn. When I looked at my history lesson, the words swam in incomprehensible rows over the page, like I was still staring at the ocean's waves.

Carol, though, got sentimental, pressing roses from the hundred bushes my parents had planted around the house in a fit of landscaping, never mind how many hours we'd spent picking Japanese beetles off those same rose bushes, dropping them into mason jars full of kerosene for the grand bounty of a nickel a jar. She shot a roll of pictures with her Brownie Starlite: the front yard, the backyard, her Flexible Flyer, which there was no point in taking to Florida where it never snowed. For her, the three weeks went by too fast, like when you stare out a car window and the telephone poles along the highway are one big blur. For me, the weeks dragged along like when you pick out one pole way up ahead, and follow it with your eyes as it comes closer, so slowly it hardly seems like you are moving at all.

We missed the Surveyor 1 launch, then four days later, Gemini 9. "We could have been right there," I said to Carol, shaking my head as we watched it blast off on TV. When I asked my dad on the phone if he'd seen the launch, he said he had been at the office all day but that he had felt it. At the time, he'd thought it was a truck turning off the highway.

The last day of school finally came. The movers parked

their Mayflower van on our lawn and loaded up all our furniture except for a double bed we were going to sleep on for four nights, then leave for Goodwill. My mother watched, impressed, as the men from Mayflower swaddled the diningroom table in padded quilts, wrapped the chairs in plastic. Army movers were not so careful: the last time, they had actually broken her couch in two. The next thing to get shipped was the dachshunds.

My mother gave Bertha and Gretel the tranquilizers the vet had prescribed, wrapping the pills carefully in balls of fresh hamburger, though she needn't have bothered. Dachshunds will eat anything. Bertha had once gotten up on the picnic table at a cookout and before we caught her had eaten half a watermelon, a plate of raw onions, and four sticks of butter. After they ate their tranquilizer meatballs, they got very sleepy, staggering around on their short, stiff legs, then toppling over, *whumpf,* like tiny beached whales.

Bertha had been our first dachshund and was still my favorite. She was a standard red, with a chest as massive and impressive as Queen Victoria's. The man who owned her mother had promised us a female, and she'd been the only one in her litter. When we went to get her, he shook his head, already regretting his decision. "She could have been a champion," he said. Bertha loved, in descending order, my father, who always walked her; my mother, who fed her;

me, who let her sleep in my bed when it was thundering or there were fireworks. She had no room left in her heart for Carol. Maybe they were too alike. Bertha had a long dachshund nose and could freeze Gretel, the younger dog, with one well-timed look down it. When she did this, to me she looked just like Carol.

If Carol was Bertha, I guess Gretel was me. Gretel's feet pointed out like mine. She was bowlegged, too, and had a goofy overbite. She loved anybody and everybody with a sort of warm, sloppy equality. She was Carol's favorite. I preferred Bertha's fierce and ordered loyalty. Even with dogs, I guess, opposites attract.

So now I knelt beside Bertha, my favorite, kissing the soft, smooth spot behind her ear, breathing her rich dog smell. She was whimpering a little. Suddenly, I didn't want to let her go. I was afraid something might happen to her. "I won't let anyone take you away from me," I whispered in her ear, hugging her. Then I let Mom put her in the big shipping crate and take her out to National Airport, like this was just a practice for all of life's small betrayals. Lucky, our cat, who my sister and I had named after the littlest Dalmatian in *101 Dalmatians,* was going to be carried on the plane.

The next day, the people in my mother's office at the Treasury Department gave her a farewell party, and she came home late from work with slices of the cake for Carol and me. Eddie, a woman from her car pool, followed her in, carrying a box of stuff from my mother's desk. She looked like she had been crying. I knew her mostly as the one who always sent us Christmas cards signed by herself and her poodle, Sammy. She hugged my mother as she left. "Think about it, Mary," she said. "It's not too late to change your mind."

My mother shook her head. "The girls," she said. "Besides," my mother waved a hand at our empty living room, "my furniture is already there."

The last thing my mother did before we went to the airport was dope Lucky, stuffing the pill down his unwilling throat and bundling him into the cardboard carrier the airline had given her. I got to sit at the very front of the plane with the cat at my feet, while my mother and Carol sat a dozen rows behind me. A woman with a small terrier in an identical carrier sat next to me. She was flying to Atlanta for her mother's funeral, she told me. I opened my mouth prepared to tell her some version of why we were moving to Florida, only to be struck by that complete sense of freedom that comes with traveling alone. I would never see this woman again. I told her I was an orphan, traveling to Florida with my cat to meet my adoptive parents. My new dad, I told her, was an astronaut.

Just then Lucky began to hiss and spit inside his cardboard cage, tearing at the cardboard with his claws. He seemed anything but tranquilized. He let loose a long yowl that left the terrier shaking. The woman scooted her dog as far toward the aisle as she could manage. She looked relieved when the plane landed in Atlanta.

After the terrier woman got off, Carol came up to sit by me. By the late afternoon, as we were circling Orlando, Lucky had pretty much shredded the cardboard cat carrier, and we were taking bets on what the stewardess would do if he got loose. Just as we landed, the cat dope he had been resisting so valiantly for the whole flight took hold, and he fell fast asleep.

My father met us at the airport. He was wearing sunglasses, pleated khaki pants, and a short-sleeved white shirt. It was the first time I'd ever seen him without a T-shirt underneath. He loaded us into the car, and we headed for the new house, which he still refused to describe. "Just you wait," he said as he drove. "You can hold out one more hour."

Outside Orlando, the land on either side of the highway turned incredibly flat. It stretched away into the hazy distance broken only by pine trees with low, umbrella-like branches. It reminded me of something, and when I realized what, I poked Carol. "Hey, look," I said, "the Dark Continent." She sat up and opened her eyes. It did look like Africa, like any minute we would see lions in the dry grass. My father took his eyes from the road for a second. He shook his head. He didn't see the similarity, but then he watched a lot less of *Mutual of Omaha's Wild Kingdom* than Carol and I did.

"Now, girls," my mother said.

Then up ahead in the veldt, something truly strange appeared. "Look," I said, pointing. My father slowed down. A road met the highway, and off it branched more paved roads, miles of roads lined by overgrown sidewalks. There were even poles for street lights, an intersection with a faded stop sign. But no houses. A complete town laid out in the middle of nowhere with no houses. It was so odd, my father braked again, slowing the car to a crawl. In front of us, mounted on top of a metal pole, was a rusty planet with two lesser balls of corrosion orbiting it. The sign said SATELLITE CITY.

"Oh, I read about this," my father said. "Seems that Kennedy planned to put the Manned Space Center out here somewhere, but Johnson put it in Houston instead, and the bottom fell out."

My mother sighed. Here was another proof that the world would have been a better place if the handsome young president had lived. She wasn't sentimental about much, but she had an affection for Kennedy, which was shared by my sister, who had hung an autographed color picture of JFK over her bed. My mother had even taken us to see him once at an Easter Egg Roll on the White House lawn. Carol had been disappointed because Kennedy's hair wasn't as red as it was in her photograph. Later, after we'd stood in a day-long line to see his grave, it was my turn to be disappointed. The eternal flame, which I had imagined as something impossible and mystical, turned out to be a sort of bunsen burner.

Carol made a face at Satellite City. "At least we're not moving *here*," she said. My father stepped on the gas. The ghost town receded.

When we got to Cocoa, my father turned onto U.S. 1. He patted my mother on the knee. "Almost there," he said. My mother lit a cigarette. I realized the house my father had picked out was going to be in Cocoa. I couldn't believe it. Instead of living across a canal from Mrs. Henry and her aqua swimming pool, we were going to live in a subdivision a half mile from the Rocket Motel. "This way I'm less than two minutes from work," my father explained. "No bridges." He looked at Carol. "If we want to go to the beach, we can just drive out there on the weekend."

We turned off U.S. 1 into a subdivision of pastel cement block houses a little like the model house on Cocoa Beach, but older, with faded paint and dry, sandy brown yards. "This is Indian Heights," my father said, though the word *heights* here in flat, sandy Florida seemed like wishful thinking, like naming an ice-covered island Greenland. We went over a big hump in the pavement that signaled the boundary between Indian Heights and our subdivision, Luna Heights, a newer one, where there were still empty lots and half-finished houses. We passed an aqua house, another that was a glistening tangerine. What color would ours be painted?

It wasn't painted any color. It was brick. Red brick with black shutters, just like our house in Maryland, or sort of. After my father pulled into the garage and we got out, I could see that the bricks on the front of the house were only one deep, laid over concrete blocks. The shutters, too, were concrete, cast onto the walls like the sea horses in the Henrys' neighborhood on Cocoa Beach.

"Brick," Carol said. She sounded pleased.

"The only one in the neighborhood," my father said. "It's expensive here. They have to haul it down from Georgia." He unlocked the front door. Bertha and Gretel came charging out, wiggling and peeing on the driveway in their uncontrollable delight, sniffing at us, at Lucky in the remnants of the carrier. I bent down to pet them, but they ran back in the house, moving much more quickly than dachshunds usually do. We followed them inside and found green wall-to-wall carpeting, identical to what my father had picked out for our house in Maryland.

"New?" my mother asked.

"I just had it put in," my dad said, sounding proud and a little nervous. "That terrazzo is hell on your feet." We followed him into the living room. My mother set the cat carrier down, opening the flap on the top, and Lucky staggered out. The air-conditioning was on, and the curtains were drawn so tight it was dark. All our furniture was there. The big green sofa and matching armchair, our piano, the cherry dining-room set. They barely fit in the Florida-size rooms. The coffee table was wedged between the couch and the piano bench. The china cabinet was so close to the dining-room table that it was clearly impossible to open the drawers.

"And I've arranged to have bottled water delivered," my father said, continuing the tour. My mother nodded. We all remembered what the water tasted like.

"The TV's in here," Carol called, from somewhere ahead of me, from what turned out to be the family room. Our big black-and-white console TV was sitting in front of a brick fireplace that took up one whole wall.

"Does it ever get cold enough here to have a fire?" My mother asked. My father laughed.

"If we turn the air-conditioning way down."

Carol was trying to get something to come in on the TV.

Since the movers had taken it away four days before, she'd longed for this moment. She twisted the rabbit ears first this way, then that.

"I can't get anything," she said.

"That's because the nearest station is in Orlando," my father said. "Sixty miles away." Carol stopped.

"You mean," she said, staring at the snow that filled the screen, "you've moved us somewhere there isn't any TV?"

"We'll have to get an outside antenna, that's all," my father said. "Everyone here has one."

The dogs were now at the backdoor, whimpering to go out, the excitement of our arrival still too much for their dachshund bladders. I opened the door and stepped outside, Bertha and Gretel brushing past my legs in their eagerness to find some grass. Our new house was built way back on the lot, maybe so the front yard would look impressive, but the backyard was barely wide enough for a sidewalk. I leaned on the chain-link fence. On the other side was a genuine orange grove. Some of the trees were dead, hung with long gray moss, but not all of them. I saw green oranges, ripe oranges, blossoms, all on the trees at once. Above the trees, the moon hung in the still-light early evening sky like the thinnest of nail parings. Only tonight, it was different. Surveyor 1 was up there sitting in the Ocean of Storms taking pictures.

I grabbed the top of the fence, about to climb over, but I

heard a strange whooshing, rumbling sound and looked up to see a truck coming down the road beside our house, spraying clouds of white smoke. To either side of it, kids were running. My age and younger. They ran through what I knew must be fields of stickers and stinger nettles without a pause, danced in front of the truck in their bare feet on the asphalt still melting-hot from the sun. Their legs were brown, their hair almost white. I couldn't tell if they were boys or girls. I wiggled my toes inside my hot black-and-white saddle oxfords, started to pull one off, but the back-door opened again. My father put his hand on my shoulder.

"That's the truck that fogs for mosquitoes," he said. "Better come inside."

TWO MONTHS AFTER I had first seen it, I saw Satellite City again. My mother had driven to Orlando to take Carol to the allergist. I was just along for the ride. The doctor inked blue lines across Carol's arms with a ballpoint pen and injected her between the lines with fluid he drew from carefully labeled bottles: *Sand. Orange Blossoms. Mildew.* Basically, the allergist said, what was in the bottles *was* Florida. After living in the state mere months, my sister was already allergic to it.

On the way back, she sat in the front seat next to our mother, looking out the window, trying not to scratch.

When we passed Satellite City this time, I saw that it wasn't completely empty. In the distance was a single house, a Rainbird sprinkler spinning in its green yard.

When we got home, my mother pulled into the garage, cut off the AC and the engine, and we went inside. "Jesus," my mother said, "it was hot out there."

"Why don't you lie down?" Carol said.

So my mother went to take a nap, something she never used to do before the move to Florida. I had developed a theory, which I expounded to my new best friend, Marly Boggs, who lived across the street. I told her the world was divided into inside people and outside people. Most kids were outside, most parents inside. In this theory, mothers were the worst. Fathers, at least, went to their offices to sit around. Mothers just sat in their houses. But in Washington, my mother had been different.

With my mother safely down for her nap, I started for the front door. Carol called to me from the family room, and I turned back. Carol was sitting on our Danish modern sofa that my mother had had covered in nubby aqua vinyl so the dogs wouldn't ruin the upholstery. Unfortunately the vinyl made already uncomfortable furniture into something more like torture devices than casual seating. Lucky was asleep next to her on the matching nubby orange chair. Carol was an exception to my theory. Kid or not, she stayed inside most of the time, folding clothes or playing cards with Mom. "Jesse," Carol said, "Mom doesn't want you going out while she's asleep."

"I didn't hear her say that," I said. School would be starting in two weeks. Any time I wasn't outside playing seemed a waste of time. Carol, after all, was only two years older than me, not old enough to give me orders on her own.

"Well, she did," Carol said. "Come in here and play cards with me." Carol wanted to play cribbage, the game my mother had taught her, which they played together for hours now. The wooden cribbage board my mother had owned since before we were born was out on the dining-room table. I didn't want to play. I always got confused and pegged backward.

I opened the family-room curtains and looked out at the orange grove behind our house. The dachshunds were in the backyard eating fallen oranges, a new bad habit they'd developed. Bertha ate the middle out of each one that fell, then let Gretel eat the skin. When they ran out of oranges, they sat and watched the trees, waiting for the wind or time to bring down another. I was hoping to see Marly or David Mize, the boy who lived next door, or any of the kids in the neighborhood. In two months, I'd gotten to know them all, along with their older brothers and their dogs.

That afternoon, no one was outside, not even a dog, no excuse for me to run out the backdoor. Just orange trees drowning in long, gray Spanish moss. "Oh, gross," Carol said, pointing. I looked up and saw that the telephone wires just outside the window were knit together by sticky spider webs. In the middle of each web was a big, furry, black-and-yellow spider. I counted to ten to prove that spiders didn't bother me, then shut the curtains.

"They looked like hairy bananas," Carol said. She was playing with the bowl of wax fruit in the middle of the coffee table, shifting the red apple from hand to hand. We used to pretend the apple and the bunch of grapes were married, the colored marbles from our Chinese checkers set their many children. Carol swished the purple grapes along the table like a Southern belle in a long skirt. "Mom didn't have to come to Florida, you know," she said.

"What do you mean, *not come*?" I said. This was obviously stupid. "I mean, what were we supposed to do? Live without a mom?"

Carol shrugged.

This was too much. I heard my mother in her bedroom, coughing. She was still awake. "I'm going outside, Mom," I called down the hall. "Okay?"

"All right, Jesse," she said. She sounded tired, dreamy.

I was halfway out the door when Carol called after me. "Mom says to keep your shoes on." I kept going. "And she means it."

Marly was on top of the sand hill, a big white dune that

stood between Luna Heights and the causeway to Cape Kennedy. So far, the sand hill had been too steep and shifting for anyone to build a house on. Marly waved when she saw me struggling up the steep side, the hot sand filling my Keds, weighing me down. She was tall and very skinny, with short brown curly hair that was sprinkled white with sand right then. Just when I reached her, she yelled, "Freefall, Captain," jumped in the air, and slid feet first down the dune. I kicked off my shoes and jumped, too, sliding to a stop next to her in an avalanche of white sand. I lay on my back, my feet buried. The sand was cool underneath and damp, and I dug my hands into it like they were crabs. I could hear Marly beside me, digging, too.

"Oh, no," I said, "a gravity wave," and began to roll like a log down the hill, faster and faster, sand flying from my hands and my hair.

This was Space, the game we'd been playing all week. We rolled off the sand hill and into the Hecks' backyard, dodging meteors that fell like so much hail. Two weeks before, standing in the street in front of my house, I had gotten to see my first manned launch, Gemini 10, and I was sure we'd all be vacationing on Mars by the time I was in high school. In the Mizes' backyard, where solar wind was so fierce you had to spin in circles, David came out and spun with us. We spun across my backyard, into the orange grove, then across the River Road and down the steep bank, overgrown with elephant ears, to the Indian River. We lay facedown on the old dock that stood leaning in the shadow of the causeway bridge and trailed our hands in the brown water. I told Marly about Satellite City.

"Wouldn't it be neat to live there?" she said. "You'd have miles of streets all to yourself to ride your bike on."

I thought about that one house surrounded by all those empty streets and empty lots, enough backyards to run for miles without a single bad dog or fence. But alone? Without anyone in the neighborhood to play with? I shook my head. It would be worse than being an only child.

5

I raced home that night in front of the truck that fogged for mosquitoes. I had put my sneakers back on, and my feet felt hot. A great white cloud of mosquito spray followed me across our yard, but I beat it to the door and ran inside.

My father was in the kitchen, and when he saw me he asked, "Do you know where your mother keeps the scissors?" I couldn't help staring at him. Of course I knew. How could he not know? It was like not knowing where the bathroom was. *Don't you live here?* I wanted to ask. Then I realized that he didn't really, not like we did. In his office he probably knew which drawer the scissors were in, or maybe he didn't. Maybe he just asked his secretary, Mrs. Cowen, like he was asking me.

"Did you hear me, Jesse?" He sounded more hurt than angry, like there was a game going on and I'd left him out.

"They're in here, Dad," Carol said, pulling out the drawer closest to the phone. Lately, she hated for anyone to get upset. "What do you want to cut?" That was the question my mother always asked. The pair with the black handles were for paper and her chrome sewing scissors weren't, though we used them for that every chance we got because they were sharper.

"A tag off a shirt," he said. Carol thought about it, then handed him the sewing scissors.

After dinner, I lay on the family-room floor in front of the big black-and-white console TV while Carol twisted the rabbit ears this way and that. All she got was snow, a moving white fog as thick as the one the mosquito truck left behind. My dad had ordered a giant silver aerial from Sears like the ones all our neighbors had up on their roofs, but so far it was still in a box in the garage. He was looking for someone to put it up. He'd graduated from West Point with a degree in engineering, but apparently this wasn't the sort of thing they had taught him to do.

Carol was trying to get *I Dream of Jeannie* for me. It was about an astronaunt and was set in Cocoa Beach. It was my favorite. Even Carol liked the idea of living near a place important enough to have its own TV show.

"There, I think I've got it," she said, keeping one hand on the rabbit ears and holding the other out, so her body would act as an extra aerial. She was right. Jeannie the Genie followed by several ghosts of herself went out in her belly dancer's costume to get Tony the astronaut's morning paper. "The neighbor is going to see her," Carol said. She was right again. He did.

"She's gonna get Tony in trouble," I said, getting into the plot, which was pretty much the same every week.

"Hey, look at that." Carol pointed with her free hand at the TV screen. "I never noticed that before." Above and beyond Jeannie's ponytailed head, at the end of this suburban street in Cocoa Beach, I saw what she saw: mountains.

"That's not Florida," she said. "There aren't any mountains in Florida." She was angry. She let go of the rabbit ears, and Jeannie disappeared. "Mountains." She shook her head. "How stupid do they think we are?"

LATER THAT NIGHT, the moon woke me up. It was full, and the light coming through the window was so bright I could see the purple flowers on the bedspread, the purple-and-white plastic flower arrangement on Carol's dresser. I was sleeping in Carol's room, in one of her twin beds. Recently I'd started being afraid to sleep alone in my own room because I thought all creatures, everything living except me, could move effortlessly through time and space. Who knew what might end up under my bed? I sat up, pushing the covers away. Carol's bed was empty, the bedroom door open. I waited for the sound of the toilet flushing in the bathroom, but the house was quiet. I got out of bed.

I called softly to her, "Carol?" I could see her standing motionless halfway down the hall.

She turned, her finger to her lips. "*Shhh.*" There was a faint blue light flickering under the family-room door. The TV. Our parents were still up.

I heard my mother's voice. "So basically, without saying as much, they said it was hopeless, that if something in civil service opens up, it will be filled from Washington. So . . . I've signed up to take the teacher's test."

"Good idea, Mary," my father said, sounding a little distracted, like he was the one trying to watch TV. "That way at least you'll be able to substitute-teach."

Carol looked at me, shook her head. "But she hates to teach," she whispered. I knew my mother had taught before. She told stories sometimes about teaching in a one-room school in Kentucky, but that was twenty years before she met Dad. She'd taught again for a year when Carol was in first grade and I was in kindergarten, before she got her job with the Treasury, but I'd never heard her say she'd hated it. It didn't sound as if she'd ever told my father she did, but she'd told Carol, told her a secret, like they were friends or something. The air-conditioning cut on with a whoosh. The cold air gave me goose bumps.

I grabbed Carol's hand. "Come on," I said, pulling her toward the front door. I was trying to be quiet, afraid Bertha or Gretel, who were probably in the family room with our parents, would start barking.

"What?" Carol said. She yanked her hand away. "Where?"

I opened the front door. "Outside."

"In your PJs?" Carol stared, unbelieving. "Mom wouldn't . . ."

"Going, going, gone." I started down the front steps with Carol following. The white light of the moon was everywhere. Mom had left the Rain Birds on and they swung in wide arcs, watering more drive than grass. Now it was Carol who grabbed my hand. I tried to pull her with me, but she dug her heels in. I ran in a circle, orbiting her, trying to make her dizzy. She was the planet, me her satellite. Around and around and . . .

"Damn it, Jes," she said, letting go. I spun off across the lawn. "Stop."

"Catch me," I said and ran. I could hear Carol right behind me.

She chased me through the Mizes' backyard, setting their collie, Arrow, barking, through the Barnses' yard. Mr. Barns spent every evening after work and every weekend perfecting his lawn, which was as flat as a green on a golf course. His damp grass squeaked under our bare feet, and I caught a glimpse of Mr. Barns standing at his bedroom window, his chest naked and hairy. Carol chased me through all the yards and onto the sand hill. The sand warmed my toes as they grabbed hold. I went on all fours, scrambling up the hill, sending waves of sand behind me into Carol's face.

Then we were on top. I stood and Carol stood beside me, both of us too out of breath to speak. In the moonlight, the sand was so white it looked like snow, like this was not Florida at all. All I could see of the houses below were their white gravel roofs, blending so well in the moonlight with the empty white sand that the houses themselves disappeared. Only the black roads were left, like suddenly we did live in Satellite City. I took Carol's hand, and this time she didn't pull away. Without a word, we ran down the slope, waiting until the last instant to push off as hard as we could in a final leap. "Ge-ron-i-mo-*oh*," Carol said, yodeling the last syllable. Then we landed, sliding, our feet digging into the sand, sand slipping cool up our pajama legs, our backs.

When we stood up and the sand poured out, something fell out of my pants leg and clinked on the road. "What was that?" she said. I bent down and picked up a piece of a Coke bottle, worn smooth by the sand. I held it out for her to touch. "There was *glass* in that sand?" she said, like she couldn't believe it.

"It isn't going to hurt you," I said. "Look, the edges are all smooth."

She wasn't listening. She kept shaking her head. "You made us run barefoot over broken glass?" I shrugged.

Carol sneezed.

So to me it seemed like Carol's fault two days later when I came sliding barefoot down the sand hill one last time before dinner, and there was a piece of freshly broken glass, brown glass, from a beer bottle maybe. I felt it cut into my right foot.

I stood up, afraid to look. "Is there blood?" I asked Marly. I held up my foot for her to see.

"There's blood," she said. I looked. Red was mixing with the white sand that clung to the bottom of my foot.

"Your mother is going to kill you," Marly said. She brushed her sandy brown curls out of her face. "You said she told you not to run around barefoot." I ran to get my sneakers from behind the bush where I had thrown them. They were almost new, still white. I'd had to beg for genuine Keds. I put my left shoe on, tied the laces. Then I threw the right one as far as I could. It turned heel-toe, heel-toe in the air, up over the fence that separated the sand hill from the causeway, and bounced twice on the asphalt shoulder. Marly looked at me like I was crazy.

"The glass went right through my shoe," I said, practicing my lie. Marly shook her head. She didn't think much of my chances.

"Your mother is still going to kill you," she said.

I limped home, leaving small moon-shaped bloodstains on the driveway. I could hear Carol in the garage, taking a load of clothes out of the dryer. I opened the front door as quietly as I could so she wouldn't hear me.

My mother was in the kitchen, having a drink before dinner. She was wearing a sleeveless top, shorts, and bedroom slippers. The dogs were sleeping under the kitchen table, snoring slightly. I leaned on the table and lifted up my foot. She took a sip of her bourbon. "Well, let's go to the bathroom and take a look," she said. I waited for her to ask me how I did it, but she just followed me, her drink in one hand. I limped extravagantly, hoping for sympathy. I heard Carol come in from the garage, start down the hall behind us, but my mother shut the bathroom door, closing Carol out.

I sat on the vanity beside the sink while my mother ran water over my foot. I closed my eyes. "I think you'll live," she said. I opened my eyes. The cut was nearly an inch long. The glass had sliced clean through my new hard callouses, the ones I had earned by going barefoot every day for a month. It looked bad, but when I bent closer I could see that the soft skin underneath was only broken at the top of the moon, where I had landed on the glass with my full weight. Already, the cut had almost stopped bleeding. My mother opened the cabinet under the sink and got out the round blue box of Morton's salt she kept there for gargling away sore throats. "Lift up your foot." She filled the sink with warm salt water. "Okay, put it back." I did as she said. The salt stung. She sat on the edge of the tub drinking her bourbon and water and watching me. She didn't say anything. I looked at myself in the mirror, which was slightly fogged with the steam from the sink. I certainly looked guilty.

"I was barefoot," I said. She nodded. "I wasn't wearing my shoes."

"Obviously not," she said. She didn't seem upset. I thought of my nearly new sneaker lying on the side of the highway. Maybe if Marly held the barbed wire apart, I could crawl through the fence and retrieve it. I decided not to tell my mother about my shoe just yet. Then she smiled at me, and I felt a question coming.

"Do you know what milkweed is?" she asked. I shook my head, confused. "It's a plant with hollow stems like bamboo"—she formed an O with her forefinger and thumb—"or a bunch of soda straws." She touched a hand to her right knee, and I saw she had a scar there, an old one, a round white lump. "I fell once and a piece of milkweed went in right here," she said. "I didn't tell anybody, and it got infected. My knee swelled up as big as a cow's. That was before antibiotics. I'm lucky I didn't get blood poisoning and die." My mother rubbed her finger across the raised scar. "My father carried me everywhere for a month. He wouldn't let me walk, wouldn't let my feet so much as touch the floor."

I didn't say anything. I just sat there. I was waiting for the point, for this story to become a lesson—that there were dangerous plants, that parents knew best. My mother just shrugged. There wasn't any point. It was just a story. She was talking to me like we were the same age, like she wasn't my mother at all. Maybe this was the way she talked to Carol when they played cards, why Carol knew the things she knew.

"I'm sorry," I said.

My mother took another sip of her bourbon and looked at me, puzzled. "For what?"

"For going barefoot when you told me not to." My mother still didn't seem to understand what I was talking about. She shook her head. Just then Carol sneezed. She was in the hall, right outside the bathroom door.

Then I understood. My mother hadn't said anything to Carol about my going barefoot. It was Carol, Carol who worried about my getting hurt, my mother's being unhappy, my father's feeling left out.

"You can take your foot out now," my mother said. "It's

soaked long enough." I lifted my foot and looked at the cut, the edges now white and soft.

"Carol's going to kill me," I said. My mother nodded, as if now we both understood. She handed me a towel, and we sat there a minute more, like we were kids hiding out. Then she opened the bathroom door and let Carol in.

6

When I was growing up, my sister and I used to joke that, for all we knew, our father could be a Russian spy. Sure, he said he'd been born in Idaho and grew up in nearby Spokane, Washington, where he once had a mother and a father and still had two sisters, but we'd never met so much as a cousin. Once, when we still lived in D.C., one of his sisters sent me a pair of gloves for Christmas, gloves too large even for my mother. The card was signed *Your Aunt Tad*. That didn't prove a thing, I said to Carol. Anybody could have sent them.

My father had been born in Rathdrum, Idaho, on January 4, 1914. He always told us the place had become a ghost town, but apparently it was merely a near-death experience, because I have been to Rathdrum, and it still exists. His fa-

ther was a successful businessman. We used to have a picture of him posed in a general store he owned in nearby
Spirit Lake, Idaho. Maybe Carol still has it. She did send me
the picture of my father as a baby on his father's lap. When
I was little, this picture used to confuse me since my father is
wearing a long, white dress, but my mother explained that
was what babies, boy or girl, wore then. In this picture, my
grandfather is handsome, obviously blond even in a black-
and-white photograph. But I can't say he looks much like
my father or like my sister or me.

The picture my sister didn't send of my father's father in
his store makes a pair with a picture of my father's mother
teaching school in Idaho, eight barefoot children posed in
front of her, four of them with the same last name. Somehow my father's parents met. Somehow they married and
had two daughters and then a son, my father. When he was
just a boy, his parents divorced. I don't know if they were
living in Spokane when this happened or if his mother
moved there with her children after the divorce. Even as a
child, I sensed this was not a subject my father wanted to
discuss, though I always wanted to ask why his parents got
divorced.

After my father died, I was struck by regret: *Why hadn't
I asked?* Now I know that whatever he might have told me
would have been, at best, only a part of the truth, the part a

boy could have known or guessed about. Probably he died still wondering why his parents couldn't stay together.

The result was that my father was raised by women, his mother and two sisters. In spite of this, he told only one story about his mother. He said that when he was a little boy, his mother dressed him in Little Lord Fauntleroy suits and fussed over his long blond curls, which she would not allow to be cut. One day, he took a pair of scissors and whacked them off himself. Then, he said, she had to take him to the barber shop for a real haircut. In another picture, he is eight or ten, with the short blond hair he earned the hard way with his scissors. Already, he has the beginnings of what he jokingly called his fine Anglo-Saxon nose, though in truth it was the kind of nose that made waiters in Miami bring him matzo balls in his chicken soup. It was his most distinctive feature, the sort of nose that only shows its true nature after adolescence, as my sister soon found out. In this picture, he looks so much like Carol at the same age, they could be the same person.

Maybe that's why every picture of my father brings out in me a feeling of fierce protectiveness. He has kind eyes, a slight smile, and gazes bravely straight out of the picture as if nothing he can think of scares him. Something in me wants to tell him to duck, to close his eyes, to spare him what is coming. By most objective measurements, he had an easy, even luxurious childhood. Listening to him talk about growing up, it was hard to believe my parents had been born in the same century, let alone the same decade. My mother told stories of watching freight cars full of destitute men roll by, about her mother leaving food on the back steps for them. My father, who went to Lewis and Clark High School in Spokane, told stories of taking fencing lessons, of swimming in an indoor pool, of French and Latin classes.

Even his adventures, his perils, were well organized. He was an Eagle Scout, a boy who earned merit badges in archery, knots, fishing, hiking, swimming, and cross-country skiing. When another kid broke his leg on a winter camping trip, my father got a special commendation for hauling him to warmth and safety on a sled built from tree limbs. In his 1932 high school yearbook there are pictures of 187 graduating seniors, smooth-faced young men with their hair parted neatly in the middle, wide-eyed young women whose hair clings to their heads in tight and careful waves.

Underneath each picture is what course the student fol-lowed: Scientific, General, Commercial, Home Ec, Manual Arts. My father was in the Classical Course. For students who were going on to college, the yearbook also lists what school they were planning to attend. The most popular choice was the University of Washington, but my father was headed for West Point, a fact almost all the inscriptions mention. *Here's to the future commander,* a friend wrote. Another: *To the General, long may he wave.* And my favorite: *Dear Eddie, when you're shooting craps with the other low lifers in the army, remember your old pal, Art.*

My father was supposed to have gone to Stanford, but his father had been hit hard by the stock market crash and the Depression. I still have a folder filled with beautifully engraved, completely useless mining stock certificates. We used to have a trunk full. At some point in my father's bachelor days, he said, he'd papered a bathroom with them. West Point was not only free, they paid you just to be there. He said he made more his first year as a cadet than a teacher earned at his high school in Spokane.

As far as I can tell, my father left for West Point at eighteen and never went home again. He was an unlikely recruit, at five foot six barely tall enough to be admitted, though he had broad, strong shoulders. He was on the swim team, which he loved, until he got a sinus infection that turned into bronchitis, then pneumonia, which, in those days before sulfa drugs or penicillin, almost killed him. In spite of being from the West, he hated horses and riding, something still mandatory at the academy, where the glory days of mounted cavalry had not entirely faded. The horse he was assigned knew my father wasn't a good rider and developed a trick of shaking his head violently when my father stood next to him in formation. In four years, the horse broke my father's nose eight times. It was broken twice more, once while boxing, once in a game of football. His already large nose developed a quite distinctive hump. During a routine checkup a month or so after the tenth break, the academy's doctor suggested that he could fix my father's nose, but to do that, he explained, he would have to break it yet again. "Wait a week," my father told him. "Chances are it'll be broken by then." But he never broke his nose again, and so it stayed quite crooked.

In 1936 my father graduated from West Point. He always said that after West Point, war was easy. In his senior picture, the photographer took the liberty of touching up his nose, and in the West Point annual for that year, *The Howitzer,* it looks straight as any ruler. Under his picture, a joking caption reads: *The Northwest grows tall trees, but not so our El Toro.* (His nickname was the Bull, for stubbornness or strength or some other, less printable attribute. Carol and I could never get him to say.) The only other picture of my father in *The Howitzer* was a snapshot taken when the cadets were away learning how to fly. This was in the days of the Army Air Corps, before there was a separate air force, and so flying was part of every cadet's training. The caption for this picture is *Fogged In,* and it shows two cadets, still oversize boys, slumped on a sofa sleeping. Behind them, my father is curled in a chair, reading. His head is circled in blue ink, and a note off to the side reads simply *Me*.

He graduated into a tiny peacetime army. The generals were aging leftovers from the last war, and the junior officers mostly boys my father's age commanding companies in which many sergeants and enlisted men were old enough to be their fathers or even grandfathers. The only stories he told about life in the army were from those days before World War II. His first command was a company of white matched mules used to pull artillery in the post parades. No matter how he tried to hide them during war games, they were always the first unit captured. Mud, brush, nothing could keep the commander on the other side from picking up his binoculars and saying, "There's that second lieutenant and his damn white mules. Go get 'em."

He got posted to the Panama Canal zone in 1938, and here his stories ran to barracks humor, like his tale of having put an iguana down some colonel's latrine. Naturally, the lizard tried to escape, only to find its way blocked by some naked section of the colonel. In the box of pictures Carol sent, I'm surprised to find a tiny square snapshot of my father I have never seen. He is standing on a hill, above some tent camp cut into the jungle. He is smiling his usual warm smile, looking gently friendly, a little bit amused. He is dressed in wrinkled khakis and looks tanned and blond, the humidity making his short-cropped hair uncharacteristically curly. Next to him stands an older sergeant who, though my father outranks him and is probably his commanding officer, stands a good head taller.

Then came Pearl Harbor. My father was a first lieutenant on leave in New York City when he heard the news. He jumped into a cab in Central Park, but the cabby was so upset when my father told him the news, he hit a tree, sending my father headfirst through the windshield. He was taken unconscious to the nearest hospital. He was dressed in civilian clothes when he was admitted, and waking up four days later, he learned that a world war had started without him. The army, not knowing where he was, had declared him AWOL. He spent the war in the Pacific, where the fighting, I know from movies and history books, proceeded from island to bloody island. He never spoke about it. He got a Bronze Star. He kept it in his sock drawer with his cuff links. He also had a box full of certificates he never bothered to turn in for battle medals.

Sometime before he shipped out for the Pacific, he married for the first time. Her name was Fern, and by the time he came back, he had a two-year-old daughter, my half sister Bobbie. The marriage didn't last. Once I did get up enough

courage to ask my father why, and all he said was that Fern
hadn't liked being alone with Bobbie for the duration. He
said, "She thought she'd had a harder time of it than I had."
He shrugged. "Maybe she had." When I was little and we
were still living in D.C., Fern and her new husband sometimes dropped off Bobbie, who was a teenager by then, at
our house for visits. They never came inside, just pulled up
at the curb long enough to let Bobbie climb out, clutching
her Teen Princess overnight case.

From these visits, I drew certain lessons about life, though
when I applied them, they didn't always fit as well as I
hoped. We didn't go to church, so when Christmas rolled
around I was always puzzled by all the stories about God,
Mary, Joseph, and the baby Jesus. Joseph was Mary's husband, but Jesus was the son of God. I decided that, like my
father, Mary had gotten a divorce. In my version, God was
her first husband, Joseph her second. Jesus lived with his
mother and stepfather, but God wasn't happy with the cus-
tody arrangements. No wonder the family had to flee to
Egypt. Even I knew that God wasn't somebody you wanted
to make angry.

I don't know what my father's love life was like before
Fern or before he met my mother. I'm sure there were other
women. He always said he had a knack for getting women
the wrong age to think that he was something special. When

he was young, he told me, it was the mothers who all loved him. Why don't you go out with that cute young Eddie? they would ask their daughters. When he was old enough to be their father or even their grandfather, the cheerleaders at the junior college would chip in to buy him a team sweater and go on and on about what a sweetie pie he was. I'd say, judging by his choice of first Fern and then my mother, he may have had a knack for picking out the wrong women even if they were the right age.

When we were children, my father told us he met my mother at a chicken dinner. She was still in the WACs then, but whether or not this was in a mess hall was never clear to me. She said she noticed him because he was polite to women officers, always returning her salute, and because he had just gotten a crew cut, which she thought looked terrible on him. There was another, darker part to the story, one I didn't learn until much later. When I was little, I just thought they'd met, seen my sister and myself in each other's eyes, and married in order to have us.

So my mother, who loved the army, left it. My father, who was always an odd match for the service, stayed in. He finally retired in 1963, when I was in first grade. The army wanted to send him to Vietnam for a tour of duty, promising to promote him from full colonel to general if he would agree to go once more to war. My father didn't want to go.

He didn't want to be away from his family for four years. He'd requested California for his last assignment, thinking to retire on the West Coast, where he'd grown up. He thought it violated some unwritten army code that they'd even asked him to go overseas again. Also, he didn't approve of the war, then still in its infancy, or the way it was going. He wasn't a George McGovern in uniform, but he'd seen what happened in Korea and had a career officer's distrust for wars that couldn't be won. He told the army to send somebody else. He'd started as a cadet at West Point in 1932, so by this time he had his thirty years for full retirement.

When he retired he received a commendation, and there was a ceremony at the White House. He brought home a picture of himself, in his uniform for the last time, shaking hands with Kennedy, the astronauts' favorite president, a man who was gung ho about sending troops to Vietnam and test pilots in rockets into cold, deep space.

7   January 1967

In Maryland, with the nation's capital next door, every grade in school had its own special field trip. First grade was the National Zoo, second the Museum of Natural History, third the National Gallery of Art, fourth the Mint, fifth the White House, and in sixth you got to go on an overnight trip to Colonial Williamsburg. In Cocoa, I thought, surely we'd get taken to the Cape. So in January, when my fifth-grade homeroom teacher Miss Davis said she had permission slips to pass out, I was sure that was what they were for. She counted off a stack and called that week's paper monitor to the front. "Just the girls," she said.

It turned out we needed our parents' permission to see some movie the next day. The boys, announced Miss Davis, would have an extra recess. I caught Marly's eye. She was still my best friend, though homeroom was the only class I had with her. This was only elementary school, but we moved from room to room and teacher to teacher for classes in English, science, and math. We were all tracked by our scores on standardized achievement tests, and, except for homeroom, were herded into little, supposedly like-minded groups. We weren't supposed to know what track we were in, but all of my classmates knew we were in the Advanced Track. One of the boys, a real pain who never missed a day of school, had even said as much to one of the substitute teachers. "We don't have to do that," he said about some spelling drill. "We're *Advanced*."

Still, you didn't have to be Advanced to figure out how the system really worked. Almost all the black and poor kids were in Basic and seemed to spend most of their school day helping the janitor. Marly was a High Regular. On the bus home, I told her I'd hoped the slips were for a trip to the Cape. "Field trip?" she said, surprised by the idea. Marly had been in school in Cocoa since first grade.

"You've never been on a field trip?" I asked.

"Nope. And I never heard of anybody taking one to the Cape. Everybody goes out there with their dads." She saw I was disappointed. "They've started up a regular tour," she said. "In buses. Want me to ask my mom if she'll take us?"

Of course I did. Marly's mother was tiny and lively and

talked even faster than me. In her case, with a Spanish accent. She even laughed with an accent. I thought she was a lot of fun for someone's mom. She'd been raised in Cuba, and she knew all kinds of strange things, like how fresh-cut aloe was good for sunburn or that you could eat the loquats that hung in yellow clusters from the trees in the neighborhood. She had come to America right after World War II to marry Marly's father, who had been her pen pal. Marly had even taken the ferry from Key West to Cuba as a little baby, before Castro. Now Mrs. Boggs sent what she could to her family there, a baby sock in this letter, three aspirin in that one. She said if the postmen in Cuba saw something worth money in a letter, they would take it. "It's not bad enough they work for Communists," she said, shaking her head. "They have to steal too." One of her brothers had swum all the way to Florida and now lived in Miami with other exiled Cubans. Mrs. Boggs was the only Cuban, as far as I knew, who had made it as far north as Cocoa.

My mother was in the kitchen when I came in from the bus stop. She was stringing green beans and singing to herself. She broke each bean in two with a crisp, authoritative snap. She dropped one, and Bertha, waiting at her feet, snatched it up, too worried about any potential competition from Gretel to realize what it was. Gretel was huddled under the kitchen table. Bertha turned and glared at her, growling, even though she hadn't moved. Lately, Bertha had begun taking their arguments too seriously, once going for Gretel's throat in a move that was no game. My mother poked Bertha with a slippered toe. "Knock it off," she said.

Then she dumped the beans into a big aluminum pot with a good-size piece of salt pork and poured some bottled water on top of them. Green beans were the only thing she made Kentucky-style, cooking them for hours just the way her mother had. That she was making them meant she was in a good mood. She was about to start a job at my school as a replacement teacher. One of the teachers in the fourth grade, some guy, had quit, and my mother was set to step in as his permanent replacement as soon as her scores came back from Tallahassee proving she'd passed the statewide teacher's test. Whatever doubts my mother had about teaching, she must have gotten over them.

I poured myself a big, cold glass of Hawaiian Punch, drained it, then wiped my mouth on the sleeve of my shirt. I handed her the permission slip. "Mrs. Boggs wants to take Marly and me out to tour the Cape," I said, sneaking two permissions into one.

"When?" she asked, wiping her hands on her apron.

"The movie or the trip?"

"The trip."

"Maybe this weekend. The movie's supposed to be to-morrow."

She nodded, signed her name. "The Cape sounds like

fun," she said. "Tell Mrs. Boggs to let me know what the ticket costs, and I'll pay her back. Or maybe"—she scratched her nose with the back of her hand—"I'll just send some money with you. I'm sure you'll want some lunch."

THE NEXT DAY after lunch, Miss Davis sent the boys out to the playground. Glancing back over their shoulders, they filed away under the watchful eye of Mr. Lewis, the math teacher. Mrs. Rim, the school nurse, marched us girls in the opposite direction, into the school cafetorium, still warm with the smell of sloppy joes. A film projector was set up, the white screen pulled down to cover the stage, and a couple of mothers I didn't know sat in chairs flanking it. I found a chair next to Marly, who had gotten there ahead of me.

"What's this all about?" I whispered, curious now.

"Shhh!" Mrs. Rim said, trying to quiet the general rush and whoosh of girls' whispering. "Watch carefully." She nodded at the mothers, "We will answer any questions you have after the movie."

I don't know what I had expected. Maybe I'd been too full of thoughts about the Cape to bother to wonder. The movie was titled *The Wonderful Thing That Is Going to Happen to You Once a Month*. It opened with a shot of a girl, Cindy, in a puffy white party dress. "Today," a deep male voice announced, "is Cindy's birthday." But something else wonderful was going to happen to her that day. She was going to become a woman. Or, as it turned out, she was going to bleed like a chicken with its head cut off.

We were shown a black-and-white outline of a woman's body. Ovaries and babies were mentioned. The outline disappeared too quickly for me to match it to my own skinny torso. The important thing, the man's voice said, was that Cindy could still have a wonderful time on her birthday even though she was menstruating, provided she didn't go horseback riding, do gymnastics, or swim in terribly cold water. Cindy's mother held up a kind of fat paper pillow, called a sanitary napkin, and showed her how to strap it between her legs with a contraption that looked more complicated than the garters my mother wore to hold up her stockings. I suddenly remembered how my mother used to keep a box of those big white pads in the linen closet outside the bathroom in D.C. How I had once borrowed one to make a bed for one of my trolls only to find it missing the next day and the box mysteriously gone as well. Now I knew why. The movie ended with Cindy, still in her spotless white dress at her birthday party, dancing with her terribly handsome dear old Dad.

Years later, when I told this story to a friend who'd grown up in a tough neighborhood in Philadelphia, she said, "That's nothing." At her school, they had followed a film like the one we'd seen with one on the dangers of syphilis, showing an apartment building where one by one the lights in the windows went out while a voice intoned, "This one went mad. This one died. This one lost her baby." So it could have been worse. Still, when the projector cut off, I was in shock.

Everyone sat blinking as the fluorescent lights blinked on, but no one else looked quite as stunned as I was. I was going to bleed like that once a month? I had had no idea. I couldn't believe my mother had any idea what the movie was about. If she'd known, she would have given me some warning. Would she be angry at me when she found out? Angry at the school?

Girls began to ask questions. What happened if you started your period and you didn't have a sanitary napkin?

You could fold some toilet tissue into your panties, one of the mothers volunteered. Or, if you were in school, go to see the school nurse. Mrs. Rim, looking particularly official in her white uniform, nodded. "You should really always carry your supplies with you," she said. You never knew when your period might start, and it was best to be prepared. You might even want to carry an extra pair of panties or a change of clothes. *Carry where?* I thought, picturing each of us moving through the halls with a change of wardrobe in a suitcase. None of the girls in fifth grade even carried purses.

I began to wonder if there wasn't some way out of this. I'd spent the year lying to get out of homework, doing as little as possible in school. Since moving to Florida, all I wanted was to be outside. Was it possible to not have periods? So far, only a few of us had to wear bras, and there certainly was no sign I was ever going to have breasts. Carol was in sixth grade, and she didn't need a bra yet either. As far as I knew, she wasn't walking around the house bleeding. But then, maybe she was. Maybe she hadn't told me. Almost everyone seemed to have secrets.

"Those pads are so big," someone said. "Couldn't we just wear Tampons?" I listened carefully, unsure exactly what a Tampon was. Not until after we were married, one of the mothers said. And that was that.

Afterward, the girls huddled together in science class, whispering. We were working in small groups, and Mrs. Sack never made any effort to mix girls with boys. We were doing experiments that involved dropping marbles into glass tubes full of some kind of thick liquid. The marbles floated slowly to the bottom like the pearls in those Prell shampoo commercials. We were supposed to be learning by deduction about viscosity, but today we weren't paying much attention.

Tammy Lightfoot said her mother always called having a period *falling off the roof*. Marsha Miller said that last year when her older sister was up on the stage at the junior high waiting her turn to give a campaign speech for class secretary, the girl running against her was standing at the microphone as her pink stretch pants turned first a little red, then bright red with blood, while the girl talked on and on about her plans for a better and more active student council. Every person in the school had seen it. Needless to say, Marsha's sister won.

"Well," said Lisa Nesbitt, a girl who sometimes wore lipstick and who I didn't much like, "that film was too late for me. I've already started."

"Was it . . ." I began. *Awful* was the word I was headed for.

"Jesse Lee!" I turned. Mrs. Sack was right behind us, her hands on her hips. She glanced down at our empty experiment sheets, then wrinkled her nose as if she could smell us. What she smelled wasn't pretty. "You know what's wrong with you, girls?" she asked loud enough for everyone in the class to hear. "You have constipation of the mind"—Mrs. Sack looked right at me—"and diarrhea of the mouth." I felt like she had hit me. Behind, I could hear some of the boys laugh, then a couple of girls, too, ones in a different group. *Traitors*. And Mrs. Sack was, too.

I could feel my face was red. If the tubes full of viscous goo hadn't been glued down, I would have hit Mrs. Sack over the head with one. She had no right to make fun of the girls in the class that way, hold us up for ridicule in front of all the boys. Yet part of me, some part of me that didn't seem to like myself much these days, agreed with Mrs. Sack and the girls who were so traitorously laughing. We were too busy talking, too busy with our bodies, to keep up with science. No wonder women weren't the ones on their way to the moon. Mrs. Sack turned away, satisfied with what she'd done.

"Oh, go sit on a stick, you old whore," Lisa Nesbitt said under her breath, pronouncing the last word like *war*. Suddenly I liked Lisa a lot better.

When I got home from school, my mother was in the living room, using the couch to fold some laundry. The dogs were at her feet, and Lucky was asleep on the piano bench, shedding cat fur on the mahogany. I told my mother the movie had been about menstruation. "Yes," she said. She *had* known. "There's already a box of Tampons under the sink in your bathroom. So we're all ready."

"They said we couldn't use Tampons until after we get married," I said, unsure exactly why this should matter. My mother laughed.

"Well, Carol certainly uses them," she said. "You can ask her about it." Carol *had* started and hadn't said a word to me about it. My mother was carefully folding towels in thirds to fit under the bathroom sinks. "You girls are lucky. When I was your age we sewed pads out of old dishrags. After I'd used one, I had to sneak down to the cellar with a bucket of water to wash it out, so my father and my brothers wouldn't see." I'd read a ton of historical fiction. Sometimes women had babies in such novels, even died doing it, but no one had ever mentioned a word about menstruation. So books were yet another source I couldn't trust. Apparently not everything made it into history. My mother looked up, a washcloth in one hand. "When I joined the WACs, I took my old pads with me, but the army issued each of us a great big box of sanitary napkins. I thought I'd died and gone to heaven." She shook her head, then handed me the stack of towels that went in my bathroom. "Here, put these away."

I put the towels under the sink. I found the small blue box with TAMPAX written on the side in flowing, soft pink letters, and took it out. Each tampon was individually wrapped in paper to keep it sterile, just like the drinking glasses at a Holiday Inn, so I couldn't tell much about it except it was rocket-shaped. Inside the box, folded over and over until it was a tiny square, was an instruction sheet. I laboriously unfolded it, revealing a vague outline of the lower half of a woman with her legs spread inserting the Tampon into some hidden cavity in her body. Was that the same place pee came from? Carol came in and saw what I was looking at. "Don't worry," she said. "It's not that bad, except for the cramps. You'll get used to it. I promise."

Later, when I was outside playing in the orange grove, I asked Marly what she thought about the whole thing. "My mom said she started her first period when she was out in the sugar fields cutting cane. No one had told her it was going to happen. She thought she'd cut herself somehow and was dying."

We climbed up through the Spanish moss, which was full of chiggers, to the very top of one of the tangerine trees. We perched, eating the fruit that grew there, which was always the biggest and sweetest. We were playing Explorer. Sometimes we explored other planets. Sometimes it was more like *Tarzan* or *Daniel Boone,* shows we'd seen often enough on TV. My name was Dostoevsky Tolstoy and Marly was Faulkner Hemingway, names we'd chosen off the spines of the *Great Books* set in Marly's living room. We chose the names because they sounded both adventurous and terribly important. There was something about *Marly* or even *Jesse* that wouldn't do.

We did not want to be boys. Marly had two brothers, and so had no illusions. The older one was a projectionist at the local theater and had a bedroom full of movie posters and soundtrack albums. The younger one lived in a room full of caged rodents and tortured us by sticking a mirror under Marly's bedroom door to see what we were doing. So she knew more than she wanted about boys. But we didn't really want to be girls either, not if that meant sitting in our bedrooms in lace socks like Lori Barns, the Barbie Queen of our neighborhood, spending the precious time after school painting our toenails or some other form of doing nothing. Like other primitive people, we thought of ourselves simply as the Humans. We read books and assumed the boys in them were not really boys, but adventurous and brave young humans much like us. "Oh," said Marly, spitting out a seed, "my mom said if you still want to go to tour the Cape, she'll take us first thing tomorrow."

MRS. BOGGS DROVE a white 1959 Buick that was in perfect condition and had fins and decorative holes in the side, like cars in a book of *New Yorker* cartoons my father had. In one cartoon, a mother bird, who has made her nest in one of the holes, is shown with worm in beak flying desperately after her open-mouthed chicks as the car speeds down the road. Mr. Boggs, an electrical engineer at the Cape, liked to fix up odd or old cars. Their other one was a Saab, a make of car no one had ever even heard of. He was also building a real one-man plane on their dining-room table, ruining the TV reception for the whole neighborhood by running power tools most evenings, not to mention forcing his family to eat all their meals on the breakfast bar in the kitchen.

On Saturday morning, Marly and I slid into the backseat of the Buick, while Mrs. Boggs got in behind the wheel and adjusted the pillow she sat on so she could see over the dashboard. She was like a miniature mom. Marly was already taller than her mother, and I almost was. Mrs. Boggs clicked her tongue disapprovingly when she saw I was wearing shorts. She and Marly both had on long pants, and Mrs. Boggs was carrying a sweater. It was a typical Florida January day, cloudless blue sky, little humidity, maybe eighty degrees, the kind of weather that fooled people who visited in winter into moving to Florida from the frozen North. It seemed perfect to me as well. For real Floridians, eighty seemed chilly. If it dipped to seventy-five, Mrs. Worthington wore a wool coat when she walked her beagle, Sir Galahad, and she made him wear one as well.

"My shirt's got long sleeves," I said to fend off any request on Mrs. Boggs's part that I go back into the house and change. I was wearing a white pressed cotton shirt with a button-down collar, a Lady Manhattan, which I had borrowed, more or less permanently, from Carol. It was my current favorite, and I liked to wear it with the sleeves rolled up. Mrs. Boggs smiled; she had a great smile. "Well, then here we go," she said, and we backed down their curved driveway.

On TV, with all the cameras showing close-ups of a smoking, soon-to-be launched rocket, the Kennedy Space Center looked densely inhabited, as if the rockets and gantries were thick as skyscrapers in Manhattan. Driving across it that day with the Boggses, at first all I saw was swamp. Except for the two-lane road we were on, the Space Center looked as Florida must have before the Spanish came, or even the Seminoles. An alligator was swimming in the ditch beside the road. A flock of white cattle egrets strolled in the tall grass.

The Space Center was on Merritt Island, that finger of land between the mainland and the beach, and not on Cape Kennedy proper, which belonged to the Air Force, though all the Mercury and Gemini shots had gone from there, as would Apollo 1. Even I, no daughter of a space flight engineer, knew that much. Soon though, all the manned flights would blast off from new pads being built here. We followed the signs for the visitors' center, passing a few low cement-block buildings that weren't nearly as nice or as new as the ones at my father's junior college. In front of one, in the middle of a sandy lawn, stood a flagpole and a couple of very tiny, barely more than flagpole-size, rockets. Still, they were rockets. It was amazing to think there were men inside those drab tan buildings planning a trip to the moon. I found the thought both scary and oddly touching, as if I'd found out the whole thing was being run by brave children still too short to reach the water fountain without a boost from their mom.

Marly pointed out the window. "That's the administration building, and over there is the astronaut training building where my dad works." The first had three stories and the second had two. As we passed, I spotted Mr. Boggs's dark green Saab in the freshly black-topped parking lot.

"He's working on a Saturday?" I said, surprised, though I don't know why. My own father had been heading out to the office as I left to go to the Boggses' this morning. Marly nodded.

"They're running some Apollo 1 tests," she said.

We parked in front of the visitors' center. "Stay together," Mrs. Boggs said as Marly and I tumbled out of the backseat and raced for the door. Inside was a Mercury capsule to peer into, the hull still blackened from its fiery return through the atmosphere to Earth. I pressed my face to the glass of the window. The inside was hardly bigger than a garbage can.

"Wow," Marly said, exchanging glances with me. It was hard to imagine someone our size inside it, let alone a full-grown man, some kid's dad, tumbling through space. Behind me I heard the clickity-clack of Spanish and of other languages I couldn't begin to guess. Mrs. Boggs heard the Spanish, too, and was soon deep in a conversation with a couple of science teachers from Madrid. We all filed into an auditorium for a quick movie about the challenges of sending men into space. Two volunteers got to taste a bite of freeze-dried scrambled eggs, just like the astronauts ate. I waved my hand like crazy, but the tour guide, a college girl, picked two cute boys her age. Then we piled onto a blue-and-white bus for a tour.

Even though it was still a cool day, the bus was baking inside. It had too many windows that let in too much Florida sun for its air-conditioning to keep up. It was a greenhouse on wheels. Someone had stuck gum in the air-conditioning vents by the seats Marly and I chose in the front of the bus, blocking what air there was. We sat sweating, waiting for the tour guide to finish checking tickets and get on board, so we could head wherever we were supposed to be going. The bus driver, an older man with a faded blue Marine Corps tattoo on his right arm, took off his hat and wiped the back of his neck with a red bandanna. Even Mrs. Boggs, who worked on her lawn on the hottest of summer days, was fanning herself with a pamphlet titled *Food in Outer Space*. "Help!" Marly said, banging on the window, trying to attract the guide's attention. She made a face, sticking out her tongue and rolling her eyes horribly. "We're burning up in here!" The tour guide frowned over her shoulder at us and took her time.

"You may have noticed we're having a little trouble with the air-conditioning on these buses," she announced over the intercom when she was finally on board and we began moving. "But we'll be getting off at regular intervals, so I hope you will all bear with me"—she glanced in Marly's direction—"and be a little patient."

Luckily, it didn't take us five minutes to reach our first stop, the Vehicle Assembly Building, which our guide said was the world's largest building. "Is tallest?" someone asked in accented English.

"Not the tallest," the guide said. "The largest. In volume," she added. She sounded a little vague about that, and since Mrs. Sack hadn't gotten to volume in our science class yet, I couldn't help her. But it was so big that when I stood next to it, one hand touching its metal skin, I couldn't tilt my head back far enough to see the top. Through the giant bay doors, tall enough for a Titan rocket to roll through, I could see men in blue jumpsuits moving across a vast concrete floor. I thought maybe they were astronauts. I asked Marly.

"I doubt it," she said. "But they are here. My dad said they were. They have their own jets they fly in from Houston just before a launch or for tests. Those are probably just engineers like my dad."

When the VAB was first built, our tour guide was saying, the building had an unexpected problem. It was so vast that clouds formed inside and it actually began to rain. They'd solved that problem with giant fans that circulated the air and blew the clouds away. Now a bald eagle, maybe confusing the building with a mountain, had built a nest on the roof. Everyone who worked at the Kennedy Space Center — she touched her own breast to include herself in that number — was proud to have on hand their own living national symbol. Besides, the Center was an official bird sanctuary. Science living side by side with nature. Now, if we would get back on the bus . . .

We all backed across the parking lot, going slowly, hoping to see the eagle and not eager to get back in our baking seats. No bird appeared to thrill us and delay boarding. "If I die, you can have my Classics comic books," Marly whispered to me as we climbed back in. We drove the length of the crawlway, the two miles of crushed rock highway that later Apollo rockets would have to creep down to reach their new launchpad, which we could see in the distance, still under construction.

Then we crossed the causeway over the Banana River, onto the sandy reaches of the Cape itself. The vegetation was browner here, and as soon as we stepped out of the bus, I could smell the salt air, hear the waves breaking on the beach just beyond the sand dunes. No wonder they had to build the VAB, a giant garage, to put together the Apollo rockets. Salt air was hell on metal. On the new boardwalk on Cocoa Beach where my dad liked to go to swim, the nails had bled great rust stains across the wood, and the heads were already popping off, leaving the boards warped and loose.

We piled off the bus at each successive empty pad, the one where Alan Shepard had blasted off, then John Glenn, Gus Grissom, the Gemini shots. They looked rusty and abandoned. Mercury was ancient history, Gemini already yesterday's news. At one, a black turkey vulture, as big as a dog, sat on top of the blockhouse. One of the cute boys who had gotten my bite of freeze-dried scrambled eggs threw a chunk of concrete at him, but he didn't move. He looked like he was waiting for something. The tour guide checked her watch. I sensed our tour was taking longer than it should, no doubt because of everyone's reluctance at every stop to get back in the oven. Even the driver seemed happy to just stand there in the shade of the gantry, watching the tourists burn up film, in no hurry to get back inside a vehicle he had more reason to despise than we did. Mrs. Boggs had drifted back to speak Spanish with the schoolteachers, maybe translating what our guide had said about this particular launch site, maybe talking about Castro and Cuba. Marly stood beside me, uncharacteristically silent and frowning.

"We'll have to hurry," our tour guide said finally, making shooing motions with her hands. "If we want to get close to Pad 34 and see Apollo 1. They're running tests this afternoon, and they'll close that road soon to buses." Then we did hurry, all of us. This was what we had been waiting for. We wanted to see the moon ship on its gigantic Titan rocket.

We were already too late. "Darn," our tour guide said when she saw the striped wooden barricades blocking the road. The bus driver started a wide, clumsy U-turn, the bus swaying as the front right tire bumped off the road into the sand. "If you'll just look out the right window . . ." our guide started, but everyone had already spotted the gantry, the tall red-and-white rocket, and piled to my side of the bus. Even at that distance, a good half mile at least, it looked huge. When it took off, the ground we were on would shake as if the Titan were a volcano. I looked over at Marly, but her eyes were closed. She wasn't looking at Apollo 1 at all.

"Are you okay?" I asked.

"I'm hot," Marly said.

"Don't worry," I said, not taking her complaint very seriously. My shirt was stuck to my back with sweat, but Marly's was perfectly dry. "You won't melt."

The bus engine revved as we finished our laborious turn, and there was an audible moan from the passengers as we headed away from Apollo 1's launch pad. Just then I saw what looked like a delivery van coming toward us, heading for the pad. None of the other passengers seemed to notice. "Marly?" I said, poking her. She sat up.

"It's them," she said. "It's the crew bus." Our bus driver honked as the van passed. Through the small rear windows I could just make out three men inside, dressed in NASA white. I waved, and the closest one raised his hands and waved back. "That," Marly said, "was Gus Grissom." The rest of the passengers, belatedly realizing the van was not full of tourists or mere technicians, rushed to the back trying to see what Marly and I had seen. Behind us the barricades across the road were moved aside for the Apollo 1 crew.

"Stop the bus," one of the Spanish schoolteachers called out. *"Por favor."*

The tour guide clapped her hands. "Now, now," she said. "That was exciting, but we have to keep going. We still have lots to see. We're heading back to the Astronaut Training Center where you'll get to view a replica of the Command Center in Houston as well as a diorama depicting astronauts landing on the moon."

Coming back across the causeway, the Space Center looked like a barely settled colony on some distant, half-drowned planet. We parked not far from Mr. Boggs' Saab and went in to see the fake control room. I knew that the real one was in Houston for no other reason than that, as a Texan, President Johnson had wanted it to be. Replica or no, Mission Control looked just like it did on TV. The far wall was a map of the world crisscrossed with lighted flight paths, flanked on either side by boards that during count-down ticked off each system as it went *Go*. I leaned on the metal railing of the balcony and imagined the noise, sweat, and cigarette smoke that must fill the real one during a launch, flight, and splashdown. I wished my father was a real engineer. I thought about Gus Grissom's sad dog-brown eyes, and wondered what it would be like to have an astronaut for a dad. Could he take you up in his private jet?

Then we went through a metal door into a large, darkened room whose floor and walls had been painted the flat black of space. On a pile of Florida beach sand was a mockup of the Lunar Excursion Module, a little aluminum travel trailer on stilts, that would take the astronauts down to the moon itself. A mannequin just like one in the men's department at Sears, but wearing a space suit, was backing down a ladder from the module, one silver-booted foot poised above the sandy surface of the moon. Our guide was talking about the benefits to mankind that space travel would bring. Already there had been such scientific progress. "If someone tries to tell you that NASA is a waste of money," she said, "you tell them that without the Space Program, we wouldn't have Teflon."

I looked up, trying to see how tall the room was. It seemed to disappear a story or two up in darkness. I wondered what it had originally been used for. I turned to ask Marly. Since her father worked here, I figured she would know, but she wasn't beside me. Then I heard a thud, and for a second I thought the mannequin astronaut must have slipped off his ladder and fallen backward onto the lunar sand. The silver man was still holding on, one foot away from being the first mannequin to leave a footprint on a planet besides ours. Then I heard Mrs. Boggs.

"*Yi, yi, yi,*" she said from somewhere behind me. Everyone swiveled. There was Marly lying on the black floor, eyes closed, arms outstretched, hands limp above her head. The sound I had heard, like a melon falling off the back of a truck, had been that of my best friend's unconscious body hitting the ground.

8

Marly moaned, her hands moving slightly. Mrs. Boggs rushed to her. I heard her knees hit the concrete floor as she knelt at Marly's side. I tried to go, too, but the tour guide grabbed me by the shirt collar and pulled me back. "Give her room," she said. A guard appeared from somewhere, then an ambulance. By then, Marly was sitting up, head between her knees, still very pale. "I think she just fainted," the tour guide said to the ambulance attendant. "But better safe than sorry." She clapped her hands to get the group's attention. "Because of the ambulance, we'll exit by the rear door," she said. "If you'll all just follow me." They did, casting glances at Marly, still sitting on the ground with her mother beside her. I hesitated, unsure what to do. If I went back to the visitor's center with the others, how would I get home? Just then Mrs. Boggs saw me and waved for me to come over.

She looked tiny, very worried. "I'm going in the ambulance with Marly," she said. "Mr. Frank"—she pointed at the gray-haired guard—"will take you upstairs. Mr. Boggs will drive you home, or, if he can't, he'll call your mother." She kissed me quickly on the forehead, then followed Marly, who was strapped onto a gurney, into the ambulance.

The guard tapped me on the shoulder. He looked about five minutes away from retirement, like maybe he was already someone's great-granddad. "This way, Missy," he said. We went through an unmarked door, climbed one flight of concrete stairs, and came out in the middle of a large room filled with metal desks. It was almost empty. "Everybody's busy with that test," the guard said. "Hope your dad isn't out there too."

"My dad?" I said. Obviously Mrs. Boggs's rapid, accented English had left him a bit confused about just who was who. "Mr. Boggs's not my dad."

"Here you go," he said, not listening to me. He pointed at a metal desk with a black-and-white name plate that read PAUL BOGGS. On one side of the desk there was a gold-framed picture of Mrs. Boggs with little curling snapshots of Marly and her two brothers stuck into the corners. The chair behind the desk was empty. "I'd better ask when he's due back," the guard said. He went away, spoke to a man in a white short-sleeved shirt and bow tie at a desk on the far side of the room, nodded, then made his way back to me. "He'll be back in an hour if everything goes as scheduled. You be okay?" I nodded. "If you need a rest room," he said, naming the one thing that in his experience all kids needed sooner or later, "there's one out that door and down the hall on the right. Don't go off this floor though. Not without no ID."

So I sat. Men came and went, none taking much notice of me. Maybe people often brought their kids out on Saturdays, on days when there were astronauts to see. I looked through Mr. Boggs's drawers, but except for some rubber bands and a slide rule there wasn't much. This was just as boring as hanging around my own dad's office at the college, where the only excitement on weekends was sneaking in to look at the urinals in the deserted men's bathrooms. I wished I could be out at the pad where the tests were being done. That would be exciting. The man with the bow tie went out and came back with a couple of cold Cokes. He set one on Mr. Boggs's desk as he passed. "Here," he said. "Your dad may be awhile. Control is taking their own sweet time on this one."

"Can I call my mom?" I asked, not wanting to explain again that Mr. Boggs was not my dad, though I thought it was pretty obvious from the family snapshots that I wasn't a curly, brown-haired junior Boggs.

"Sure," he said, scooting Mr. Boggs's phone across the desk toward me. "Push this button, then dial nine and the number. Come get me," he nodded at his desk near the far wall, "if you have any trouble."

I tried the house, but there was no answer. My mother might have taken Carol to the library, or they could have gone grocery shopping, or they could just be out shifting the Rain Birds around the yard. It was hard to say. I tried the junior college. Usually there wasn't anyone at the switchboard on Saturdays, but I didn't have any better ideas. I let it ring a long time, playing with Mr. Boggs's slide rule while I did. I had no idea how to use it, though my father had one in a box of old stuff in the hall closet, and sometimes I'd played with that one, too. I wondered what grade you were in when you finally found out what they were for. Someone finally answered, a man. Usually the girl at the switchboard said the name of the college, but whoever this was just said, "Hello? Who is this?"

I said my name, asked if he had seen my dad around.

"Just a minute," the voice said.

After a long time, my dad came on. I told him what had happened, and he said, "I was in a meeting, but we're taking a late lunch break right now. I'll come and get you, but you'll have to give me a better idea of where you are. Does the building have a number?" I called over the man who'd given me the Coke. He and my dad chatted for a while. When he hung up, he looked at me and laughed.

"I took a course from your dad when I was a cadet at the academy," he said. "If all the teachers had been as kind as he was, I might have made it out of there." I'd forgotten my dad had ever been an instructor at West Point. All his life before I was born seemed kind of vague to me. "You look like him except for that," he said, touching my still rather small nose with his index finger. I blushed. People said all the time that Carol, whose nose was already starting to grow, looked like my dad, but no one had ever said it to me.

I drank my Coke while I waited for my dad. My stomach kept growling. I'd hardly had any breakfast, and no lunch, and now it was after two. By the time my father arrived, it was nearly three. When he walked in the room, I was struck by how much he still looked like a colonel, broad shoulders held straight, hair cut short. He gave the impression of being in uniform even though he was wearing weekend clothes, a short-sleeved white shirt and no tie. I waved and rushed over, and he put his arm around me. He shook hands with the man who'd been his student. "Come back sometime when we're not so busy, Colonel," the man said. "I'd be happy to show you and your family around."

When we got outside and into my father's Plymouth, he smiled at me and said, "Hungry?"

I said, "Starving."

He turned out of the parking lot headed east, toward the beach, and I started to say something—he was famous for having a bad sense of direction—but it turned out he knew where he was going. We left Cape Kennedy and drove down Highway A1A into the town of Cape Canaveral, which hadn't, I guess, felt like changing its centuries-old Spanish name because of a dead president, no matter how beloved. He pulled up in front of a restaurant called the Moon Hut, whose façade was a full moon with a door cut in it, and whose sign was another full moon with a bamboo hut perched on the rim, as if the people who ate there were natives living on the moon.

I followed my dad in, trailing a little. The place was full of men who looked like him, that is, like military or ex-military. I saw a half dozen hands with heavy, gold West Point class rings like the one my father always wore. The waitress brought us big, stiff menus. All the sandwiches were named after astronauts or rockets. Some were obviously jokes. A Gus Grissom was a French dip, a reference to the Mercury flight where he'd opened the door of his capsule too early and it had sunk in the Atlantic, almost taking him down with it.

I didn't really like roast beef, which we had all the time. My mother bought it cheap at the commissary on Patrick Air Force Base down toward Satellite Beach where she shopped once a month. When I remembered how Gus Grissom had waved at me, one hand lifted in the air in what was very nearly a salute, I ordered the sandwich anyway. My father had a Cosmonaut, a reuben on dark rye. While we waited for our food, I told him I was worried about Marly.

He nodded. "She probably just forgot to eat her breakfast," he said, unimpressed by a little bloodless fainting. I wasn't convinced. Marly had odd tastes in food—she liked to drink orange juice while eating dill pickles—but I was the one who usually skipped breakfast; she always ate a bowl of Captain Crunch and at least a couple of strawberry Pop Tarts. Besides, it seemed an odd thing for my father to say since he often skipped breakfast, unlike my mom who needed a soft-boiled egg and toast every morning to keep her two cups of coffee company.

Just as the waitress brought our plates, I realized I had to pee and got up to find the bathroom. On the way back, I heard one of the men at a nearby table say, "Look at that. I wouldn't let my son wear his hair that long." I looked around. I was the only kid in the place. He was talking about me. In my shorts and button-down shirt, he thought I was a boy. I suddenly felt like I was in costume, like I wasn't myself at all. I sat down across from my father, wondering what it would be like to be his son instead of his daughter. Would we spend more time together?

Then my father started talking. He had been at a board meeting all morning because there was big trouble at the college. Money was missing, a lot of money, and Dr. Henry seemed to have something to do with this. Though whether my father and the board thought he'd stolen the money or just made foolish and unauthorized expenditures was unclear. Now, he had left town. Maybe for his father's funeral, but nobody was quite certain. The newspaper was onto the story now, and the board had to act. They didn't feel they could put off a decision until Dr. Henry reappeared. I thought about Mrs. Henry, Lucille, alone in her turquoise house on Cocoa Beach except for Max, their beagle. Did she know where her husband had gone or what he'd done?

"They're going to fire him," my father said. "I don't see any way around it. I'd hoped they could wait, but now . . ." He ate one of his french fries, bite by meditative bite. "I think they're going to ask me to be acting president." He shook his head. "I don't know. Do you think I should say yes?" My father looked up at me, waiting quite seriously for my answer, and I realized I didn't feel at all like his son. I felt like my mother or maybe his secretary or some other grown-up woman.

I thought about it. "I think you'll do a great job, Dad," I said. He smiled.

"The chairman asked me what I'd say if the board voted to appoint me. I told him, like Truman, I would serve if asked." My father wiped his mouth, looked around the Moon Hut, which even at this odd hour was very busy. "This place really does a business," he said. "Maybe if we stay around here, I'll get a partner and start a place like this. There's hardly anywhere to eat. A place with steaks, drinks, good desserts. A lot of bachelors work at the Cape who must eat out every night."

I looked around. It was hard for me to tell if the men around us were single or married, though I noticed the wait-resses seemed to know most of them. As I watched, one waitress stopped to put an arm around a man, to laugh at a quick joke before setting down a cup of coffee. "You want to own a restaurant?" I asked. It was my mother who had run mess halls in the army, and I couldn't imagine my father ordering menus or training fry cooks.

"Well," he said, shaking his head. "Just an idea. You know my father was a businessman, and I guess I've always wanted to prove I could be one too."

I looked at him, waiting for him to remember that his father had lost everything in the Depression, had spent his last years before he died of stomach cancer writing letters to his congressman protesting fluoridation of the water. "It's okay, Dad," I reached over and patted his hand, feeling less like his wife now than his mother. "You run a college."

My father took me home. After a quick word with my mother, he headed back to the office for the board meeting that would decide Dr. Henry's fate. The lights were off at the Boggses' house, both cars still missing. After dinner, which I ate in spite of having eaten my whole Gus Grissom, I went to my room and tried to remember what I'd seen at the Cape well enough to write it in my diary. I'd been trying to keep one off and on since Christmas, but I found my life so boring, I usually wrote nothing in it but lies. I tried to stick to the truth this time, though I ended up shaking hands with all three astronauts. Just waving as they drove past seemed insufficiently dramatic.

A little after eight, I heard Mrs. Boggs's Buick bump into their driveway. Bertha and Gretel heard, too, and scrambled barking for the front door. I ran outside. Mrs. Boggs got out, followed by Marly. "I'm going to go get your brother," Mrs. Boggs said, heading across her perfectly kept green lawn toward the Mizes'. "It's past his bedtime."

Marly walked down the driveway toward me very slowly. "So?" I said. She stopped in front of me and shrugged.

"I fainted."

"Just fainted?"

"The heat and . . ." she said, looking down at her sneakers, "I started my period."

"You fainted because of that?" I found this unsettling news.

"Apparently it's not all that uncommon," she said.

I looked at her. She had her hands on her hips, and her skinny arms stuck out at the usual sharp angles. Her hair was a curly, uncombed mess. She didn't look any different. She hadn't suddenly grown breasts or anything. "So how do you feel now?"

"Okay," she said, tugging at her jeans. "But wearing this pad is like walking around with a couch between your legs."

"What would happen," I asked, struck by an awful thought, "if you were an astronaut and you got your period in space?"

"I don't know," Marly said, shaking her head. "I mean they take care of all that other stuff, pee and all. Some astronauts even throw up. Why should this be any different?" She looked unusually subdued, as if she didn't quite believe it. We both looked up at the moon, hanging big and orange just above the river. In spite of its size, it looked farther away than ever. At least for us. It hadn't been a woman dummy astronaut backing down that ladder from the Lunar Excursion Module to the moon.

Just then the front door of my house flew open, and Carol came running out. "There's been a fire," she called to us. She had her transistor radio in her hand. She'd taken to walking around the house with it pressed to her ear listening to WRKT, Rocket Radio, the local Top 40 station.

"Where?" I said. I was hoping she would say at school, because I suddenly remembered I hadn't brought home my science book. We had homework.

"The Cape," she said. "Apollo 1." She turned up the radio. The announcer could barely speak, he was so upset. A spark had ignited the pure oxygen in the capsule. The tests had not been going well, tempers were short, when the technicians in the blockhouse heard one of the astronauts say, "We have a fire in the spacecraft." The heart rates for all three of the crew shot off the scale. Unofficial reports said all three astronauts were dead. They cut to some worker at the Cape, who could have been one of the men in Mr. Boggs's office or Mr. Boggs or anybody's dad. He had obviously been crying. "I ran to help with the hatch, but we couldn't get it open. All I could see was smoke. One of the crew said, 'Get us out of here. We're burning up.' Then the intercom went dead."

"Turn it off," I said, and Carol did. Marly and Carol and I stood there on the driveway, not saying anything, trying not to look up at the moon, so bright and orange it, too, looked like it was burning. I felt like maybe we should all be crying. But we weren't.

9   April 1967

I was on the highest platform of the tree house. Then I was on the ground, trying to breathe while people asked, Can you hear me, Jesse? Do you want a glass of water? Silly, worried questions. Then someone asked me why I fell, and I heard myself saying something about a branch that pulled out of the tree. As I said it, it seemed true. I could see a rotten branch like the arm of a Barbie doll popped from its socket, a round, useless stub. All I could really remember was the moment when my heart turned over, when I knew I had lost my balance.

At this point, my mother arrived. She had been moving the Rain Birds in our yard and was wearing old shorts and tennis shoes. I tried to sit up, but someone wouldn't let me. Then the ambulance arrived. All I could think about was how stupid this was, how embarrassing. On my report card, the school counselor had written that for a fifth grader I tested remarkably low on the manual dexterity index. I'd been working hard ever since to live down a reputation as a klutz. This was part of why I went so high in the tree house. I couldn't believe my bravery had turned out so badly.

"Forty feet," Mrs. Boggs was saying over me. "She must have fallen forty feet."

"Three stories," someone else said. "Isn't that more like thirty feet?"

The ambulance attendants strapped me to a board, lifted me up, but the wheeled gurney got stuck in the sand, and they had to carry me to the ambulance. My mother got in with me. Someone had run to the house and gotten her purse for her, but I knew she wished she'd had time to change her clothes. I wished Carol were there, but she was still at school, at chorus practice. I wondered who would go to pick her up when she called and Mom wasn't home.

The attendant put an oxygen mask on me, and because it was made to fit an adult, it covered not just my mouth and nose, but most of my face. So I couldn't see much, but I knew we were headed out of the neighborhood when I felt the bump in the pavement as we crossed from Luna Heights to Indian Heights, from our subdivision to the next. Even with the oxygen mask over my face, I could barely breathe.

My mother sat on a bench by the window, holding on as the ambulance turned onto U.S. 1 and picked up speed. The ambulance attendant held my hand. "Take a deep breath," he said. "Let it out."

"It's better," I said, "if I breathe kind of shallow."

I had been up in the tree house so high and alone because when I went after school to get David Mize, whose tree it was, his mother was yelling at him. David was a year older than me, a sixth grader, and it seemed he was supposed to take a big test in American history. He didn't. Instead, he'd asked the teacher's permission to go to the bathroom. Then he didn't come back. I imagined him sitting in one of the stalls, bored, scared, waiting for school to be over. It reminded me too much of my own life at school.

Just that week, I'd spent half an hour searching for a blue notebook I told Mr. Martin, my math teacher, had my homework in it. I told him I had lost it. But I didn't even have a blue notebook, and Mr. Martin knew it. Even my homeroom teacher, Miss Davis, whose history class I had to interrupt to search through my desk, knew it. I wanted to look like Miss Davis one day, wear matching monogrammed gold earrings and sweaters, so her knowing I was a liar hurt. I kept on pretending to be looking, digging through the mess in my desk, sweating and feeling sick at my stomach.

So I couldn't stand it when I heard David was in trouble, too, couldn't stand hearing his mother say how disappointed she was in him, using exactly the same puzzled, hurt tone my parents had taken to using. "Were you trying to get attention? Is that it?" she asked him.

"No," he said. I believed him. If he felt like I did, all he wanted was to be invisible, to disappear.

I went into the Mizes' backyard and climbed up to the tree house, which was really just sheets of plywood nailed here and there in the tree, and waited for David to come out. The tree was a live oak, huge, covered in mistletoe and Spanish moss. It loomed like a skyscraper over the orange trees in the neighborhood yards. Eventually David came out and stood at the base of the tree. Just seeing him made me uncomfortable again. Why did he skip the test? Why didn't I do my math homework? There didn't seem to be any good answer. "Hey," I called out to him, starting up to the highest platform where David went all the time, but where I had never been. "Watch me."

THEY ROLLED ME into the hospital in Cocoa and then back out again because there wasn't an orthopedic surgeon there. "We'll have to go out to Cape Canaveral," the ambulance driver said to my mother.

I felt us fly up and then down the high bridges Carol was

so afraid of. "God," my mother kept saying. "Christ." She was not praying but looking out the front window, watching the cars that the ambulance had to dodge. The driver hit the siren time and again, but no one moved.

"Half the time, with their windows up and the AC on, they can't hear it," the attendant said. "And the other half . . ."

"Where are the police?" my mother asked. "They should all get tickets." One thing my mother believed in was the law. She had already lectured me twice about not answering chain letters, and once, after I put my initials on some quarters with purple nail polish, about defacing government currency.

Cape Canaveral Hospital was in the middle of the Banana River, on a part of the causeway pumped up from the river bottom. The attendant and the driver had me out in a minute. Acoustic ceiling tiles flew by above as they wheeled me into the emergency room. My father was there. A neighbor had called. He had driven from the junior college and somehow had beaten us. "Thank God," my mother said. "At the first hospital, they took one look at me dressed like this and wouldn't believe we had insurance."

Now, instead of ambulance attendants, there were nurses. They looked scared, and suddenly I was, too. When one of them told another to cut my shirt off, I started to cry. It was a bright green Hang Ten shirt from Ron Jon's Surf Shop on Cocoa Beach. I had begged for months to convince my mother to take me there to buy it, and I had worn nothing else since. My mother had already washed it twice that week. I asked the nurse to let me sit up so she could pull it off over my head, but she ignored me. I heard the curved scissors cut through the cloth.

I was so upset I made the mistake of taking a deep breath, or trying to. The pain made everything in the room go black for a second, like when you flicked off the TV then turned it right back on. "Please," I said, "give me something to kill the pain." This seemed like a line from a movie or TV, and it embarrassed me to say it, but once I started I couldn't seem to stop. "Something to kill the pain." I saw the stricken look on my mother's face, on my father's, and I wanted to shut up but I didn't. "Please . . ."

A doctor leaned over me, put his hand on my forehead, and brushed back my hair, which was full of sand from the Mizes' backyard. He had a dark tan and a beard like a sultan. "Jesse," he said, looking at my chart. "Glad to meet you. I'm Dr. Barsamian." I nodded as best I could. "Listen, my Jewel, we can't give you anything for the pain until we're sure you don't have a concussion. Okay?"

"Okay," I said. He unstrapped the back board but left it in place under me on the table.

"I don't want to move you any more than we have to, so I've sent for a portable X-ray machine, okay?"

"Okay."

He patted my head. "Good girl," he said.

The X-ray woman shooed everyone else out of the room and put on a lead apron. She inched the cold X-ray film under my back. "Take a deep breath," she said. I took a shallow one. "Let it out. Stop *breeeaaathing.*" The machine hummed, and then the woman came forward to replace the film and we did it again. My head, my neck, my back, my legs.

I lay there worrying, thinking about how this fall changed the future, my mental list of what's next. I almost certainly would not have to go to school tomorrow. Even if Mr. Martin talked to my mother about my missing math homework, she would not get mad at me, not after this. That much was obvious. Did this also mean I would not get to play Mary Mary Quite Contrary in the spring PTA play? I had just been cast in this small part, and my mother had already bought yards of flowered gingham to sew for my costume. Carol was to play Cinderella. The kids in these plays got excused from a lot of classes. I'd tried out for the Christmas play, but my teachers said they thought it would be too distracting. Getting okayed for this one seemed like a good sign. Even as I worried, I realized these were not very big things to be worrying about, but maybe the mind works that way. You die and your last thought is, *I guess we won't be going to Howard Johnson's for all-u-can-eat clams.*

I lost track of what was going on. Dr. Barsamian came back and ran a spiked wheel, like the one my mother used to mark dress patterns, up and down the inside of my foot. Can you feel that, Jesse? That? I could. At some point I got moved from emergency into a room for the night. A sign over the bed said PATIENT MUST BE FLAT ON BACK AT ALL TIMES.

Dr. Barsamian wanted me near the nurses' station, and so I was not on the children's ward. In spite of this, my room-mate was a two-year-old girl. She had smashed her elbow falling from a dresser. Her mother explained to my mother that the thumb they had up in traction was the one she usually sucked. The girl screamed and screamed, looking at the thumb dangling unreachable above her. After a while, my father left, then my mother, and then the girl's mother. The girl kept crying, her voice hoarser but just as loud.

Even though I had finally been given a whole lot of codeine, I couldn't sleep. I kept losing track of time, thinking: *When was the last time I breathed?* Panicking when I couldn't remember. Each moment was like waking up from a very deep nap on a hot summer afternoon and having to fight to remember where you were and who you were. Then the next moment, it started all over again. The girl stopped crying for a while, then woke and started again.

When I did start to drift off, I tried to turn on my side,

which is how I usually slept, only to catch myself. Lying on my back, I felt vulnerable. I felt like I still couldn't breathe. Sometime during the night I got sick, maybe from the codeine, maybe from the shock. It is pretty terrible to have to lie flat on your back and throw up. I was afraid I would choke. A big black nurse, Mrs. Moore, brought a little kidney-shaped pan for me to throw up in and held my head to the side while I did. Her palms on my forehead were cool and pink. The little girl was finally asleep, making restless, sucking sounds.

10

The next morning I found out I had collapsed a lung, broken a few ribs, and turned five of the vertebrae in my lower back into so much bone powder. But I was very lucky. Because of the way I fell, my spine was intact. Dr. Barsamian decided that, instead of putting me in a body cast, he would have me fitted for a back brace. This was something new and had never been done on such a young patient before. Talking to me about it, he was clearly excited.

The man who came to fit me for the brace was also enthusiastic. It would be the smallest brace he'd ever made. My chest was only twenty-five inches around. After he took measurements, he asked me what color vinyl I wanted the pads to be. "Pink?" he suggested. I shook my head. "No,

white," he said. "White's the ticket for a little lady like you."
After the first night, I was not in pain. My lung popped back
into shape. My back never hurt at all. I had a hard time believing anything was wrong with me. I felt guilty, like I was
faking it, like I had held the thermometer to the lightbulb
and convinced my mother I had a fever too high to go to
school. Maybe this was why, even when I needed to pee
really badly, I didn't like to call the nurse. My favorite nurse,
Mrs. Moore, the one who held my head the first night, told
me I had the wrong attitude. "Honey," she said, shaking her
head, "squeaky wheels get all the grease."

After it became clear I would be in the hospital for at least
three weeks, my mother quit the teaching job she had only
just gotten. Now the principal had to find a replacement for
her, too. At first she sat in the chair next to my bed all day
every day. I didn't have much to say and, it turned out, neither did she. We tried not to look at each other, but there
wasn't much else to look at. I was uncomfortable realizing
how uncomfortable we were. So I read or napped. She
bought a needlework kit and sat stitching a pattern in green
and yellow yarn. Though she used to make all our clothes
when we were little, I had never seen my mother do anything even vaguely craftsy. After quitting her teaching job, it
seemed like she didn't know how to fill her time.

After a while, she came only in the afternoons, each day a
little later. I found myself listening for the sound of her heels

clicking down the hall—the nurses all wore silent rubber soles. Her coming broke up the day, but mostly I wanted her to arrive, not to stay.

In the evening, my father came and we watched TV. Watching TV was what I usually did with Dad, so this felt more normal than sitting all day with my mother. Sometimes Dad got Cokes from the machine in the visitors' lounge. Then it was almost like a party.

The one person I wanted to see, I couldn't. Carol wasn't allowed. The hospital rule was NO VISITORS UNDER 16. So at twelve, Carol wasn't nearly old enough. Neither were David and Marly, my neighborhood friends, or my new school friends Mark Lish or Joanna Fosbleck. The closest they got was when my mother delivered a big brown envelope of letters from my fifth-grade classmates. Letticia Fuller, a shy black girl whose desk was near mine, had glued a seashell to her letter, and this made the envelope mysteriously heavy, made the letters impossible to keep in a stack. *Sorry you fell from a tree,* they said with few variations. So few, I suspected Miss Davis of writing this line on the board. Some of my classmates admitted, *I am writing you because the teacher is making us.* Not even Mark or Joanna had much original to say. Eddie Faubert, a boy who had never said a word to me, was the most honest. He wrote, *You sure must be stupid to fall out of a tree.*

At first, I was fed by IV. Clear liquid ran from a glass bottle down a tube into a needle that was stuck in my arm. The nurse told me the liquid was mostly just sugar water, and I imagined that it tasted like flat 7UP. After a few days I got to have Jell-O and real 7UP. After about a week, I got to eat soft foods like scrambled eggs and mashed potatoes. One night as a special treat, I got to eat my dinner on a gurney out in the hall by the nurses' station. I was mostly moving my meal around on my plate when, over the intercom, a woman complained from her room.

"Is this lamb? It says in my chart I can't eat lamb," she said. I had never had lamb, which was not one of the things my mother cooked, so it was a good thing she was not asking me.

"It's roast beef, Mrs. Wallace," the nurse at the desk said.

"Then how come it's gray?"

"Beats me," the nurse said and snapped off the intercom.

People started to send get-well gifts, and to keep them from sending stupid things, I made up a list of the Hardy Boy mysteries I didn't have and gave that to my mother. Soon I had a complete set. Before I broke my back, I had read only a couple of Hardy Boys, ones that I'd inherited from Carol. When I first learned to read, I made a big point of fighting the school librarian's restrictions on which books we could check out. I didn't want to read picture books. Finally my father sent a note, and the librarian had to give in.

Freed from the ABC shelves, I began to pick out books by their size alone, the fatter the better. I had read a book about a blind pony set out West on a butte and had no idea what that was or that it wasn't pronounced *but*. I read *Les Miserables* and didn't have any idea how to pronounce that. At some point, I don't know exactly when, I found myself checking out fat books but not reading them. I would just keep them for a while and pretend I had read them. I told my father I'd read *Moby Dick*.

In the hospital, though, I had to hold the book in the air over my head to read, and that ruled out anything heavy. So it was the perfect excuse for light reading like the Hardy Boys. I even read a Nancy Drew someone mistakenly bought for me. I disapproved of her. When she got into trouble she always had to be rescued by some boy.

I developed a big crush on Joe, the younger Hardy Boy, though basically he was indistinguishable from Frank, the older brother, except for his blond hair. I especially liked in *The Mystery of the Hidden Cove* when Frank saw Joe unconscious on the rocks of the bay far below. I read that scene over and over. Maybe it was just that falling from a height was something Joe and I had in common, but I sensed something exciting about Joe's blond prone body. At night, though, I sometimes dreamed about dark-haired, older Frank.

After the first night, they had moved the little girl with the broken elbow out of my room. Her parents, sorry their daughter had kept me awake, brought me a *Reader's Digest* condensed book that had both *Heidi* and *Hans Brinker and the Silver Skates* in it. Then I had a whole series of roommates, all adults. The best was a woman bus driver who could vomit a solid stream from her bed halfway across the room to the trash can. When the vomit hit the metal trash can, it sounded like a garage door being violently hosed down. The boys in my class would have loved it.

The worst was a woman who complained endlessly all evening into the intercom, "I've got to have something to drink. The doctor said I could have something to drink," while the nurses grew increasingly short.

"You know Dr. Price says you can only have two ounces of alcohol a day, Mrs. Johnson, and you've had them."

"I've got to have . . ."

Around midnight the head nurse came in with a can of beer. "Here," she said, "don't keep everybody up all night."

Then there was Regina Tipaleg. REGINA TIPALEG—the orderly rolled his eyes as he wrote it on her Styrofoam water pitcher with a black Magic Marker. He told me that Regina had had her stomach pumped for an overdose of barbiturates. "So don't bug her," he said.

After a while, Regina's mother came to visit her. "Forget it, Regina. He's married." Regina started crying.

Then a coworker: "He wants to see you. You'll have to see him sometime." She kept crying.

And then the man referred to. From the way he called her Regina and she called him Mr. Forrestal, I guessed he was her boss. He came in late in the morning, when visiting hours were almost over. "I'm sorry, Reg. You know I am, but there's nothing I can do." I waited for Regina to do something, throw her water pitcher, cry again, but she didn't say a word. After he left, she turned on the TV.

"Do you watch soaps?" she asked me. When I said no, she started explaining the show that was on. Who was who, who they were with, and who they used to be with. Behind all the on-screen coffee drinking was a whole hidden history of adulteries that had led to weeping, divorce, even suicide. "You can learn a lot watching soaps," Regina said. She was right.

One morning, Mrs. Moore was timing me while I breathed this medical fog from a respirator. "Seven minutes to go," she was saying when the bed started to shake. "Oh, honey," she said, "that's the shot." Since the Apollo 1 fire, all manned missions were on hold, so this was another unmanned Surveyor flight. Marly had told me her dad scratched her name on one of the circuits. Now *Marly* would be flying to the moon while I was flat on my back in bed.

Mrs. Moore jumped up from the chair by my bed and opened the curtains. All I could see was the top of the flag-

pole and a rectangle of sky. The river was down there somewhere, but flat on my back I couldn't see it. "There!" she
said, pointing to the far corner of the window. "There!" I
couldn't see anything. The roar got louder and louder, even
louder than it was at home. The glass in the window rattled.
"Can you see it?" Mrs. Moore shouted. I started to pull off
the respirator mask to say something, but Mrs. Moore
shook her head, pointed to her watch. "Six more minutes."

AFTER TWO WEEKS, my back brace came, white vinyl and
all. The brace man put it on me. The aluminum frame fit
tightly around my back and across my chest and hips. He
pulled the spring latch forward until it clicked into place. I
had to wear it all the time. He showed me a tiny silver pad-
lock to go with the latch. "You won't need this, will you?"
he said. "It's adults you can't trust, that you have to lock in."

Dr. Barsamian stopped by. He was very proud of me, of
the way I was healing. "You're gonna be famous, my Jewel,"
he said, knocking on the front of my new aluminum chest.
"I'm writing this up for a medical journal. I'll send you a
copy."

The day before I got out of the hospital, Mrs. Mize came
to visit and brought me a book of crossword puzzles. "So
why did you fall?" she said, after she was sitting in the chair
next to my bed. "Were you doing something stupid?" I re-

peated what I seemed to remember, about the branch coming off in my hand. "David looked all over," she said, looking at me very closely. "He found some little branches that you might have broken on your way down, but he didn't find a big rotten one."

I could imagine David doing just this, his mother yelling at him from her bedroom window. "Maybe it fell on the other side of the fence," I said. "By the highway."

She shook her head. "He looked there, too."

I didn't know what to say. Maybe, even as I lay on the ground, I made up the part about the branch, to make myself seem less stupid, less wretchedly clumsy. I felt a hot wave of guilt. Mrs. Mize stood up to leave. "Think about it," she said. "It could be important for the insurance."

When I told my mother what Mrs. Mize had said about the insurance, she frowned. "She can go to hell," my mother said, and sounded like she meant it.

On May Day, I got to go home. I went the same way I came, by ambulance. Even though it had been three weeks since I fell, I was still not allowed to sit or stand or even roll over, so getting into my parents' car would have been tough. Mrs. Moore gave me the PATIENT MUST BE FLAT ON BACK AT ALL TIMES sign from over my bed to take home with me. "Just a few more weeks," she said. "Then you can throw darts at it."

When the ambulance pulled into the driveway, Carol was standing there dressed as Cinderella in pink-and-white satin, and next to her was David, Prince Charming in blue silk. I had forgotten all about the play, which it turned out was the next night. They were on their way to dress rehearsal. Carol told me Mom gave the fabric for my Mary Mary costume to Lori Barns, who was my size and who actually was Quite Contrary, a real pill. Looking up at her from the stretcher, I thought Carol looked odd and surprisingly short. David, too. It was not the fancy dress clothes. Their faces seemed soft, almost unformed. They used to look normal to me; now, after spending so much time with adults, they looked like children. Carol patted the side of the gurney. "See you later?" she said, as if she was not sure. I nodded, suddenly shy.

Then I was back in my own room, only it was different. The furniture had been rearranged to make way for a hospital bed and a small black-and-white TV one of the neighbors had sent over. My mother fixed my favorite meal for dinner: fried chicken, cantaloupe, and blueberry muffins made from the kind of mix that had the little can of real blueberries in it. She knew it was my favorite because she asked me. I also listed my second and third favorite meals, so I could have these on subsequent nights. I couldn't seem to chew the chicken, and when Dr. Barsamian stopped by to check on me the next day it turned out that, on top of everything else, I had broken my jaw. A hairline fracture. Overlooked until now.

"I'm afraid, my Jewel, we have to keep that jaw from moving for a few weeks or else it will never heal."

"What if I promise not to talk?" I asked. "Even under torture?" Dr. Barsamian laughed, then wired my mouth shut.

So when Carol came into the room to talk about her day at school, I could only nod. She would sit watching my TV for a while, then get bored and wander out. All this should have bothered me, being alone so much, not being able to talk to Carol or anyone, but mostly it was like I was still in the hospital. Only now I got all the milk shakes I wanted, along with anything else that would turn to liquid in a blender. I got to stay up as late as I wanted, and I did, watching TV right up until sign-off. So it was like being an only child or living alone.

Finally, Dr. Barsamian announced that in just three more days I could sit up, perhaps walk around the room a little. He would come to supervise this personally. He wanted me to know I would have to take it slow because after six weeks my legs were bound to be weak, and I would be dizzy.

Late that night, after even the late movie was off, I turned on the light. I rolled onto my side, and then slowly, slowly I sat up. I braced myself with both hands and waited. I sat there listening to the air-conditioning humming and, beyond that, my mother snoring. I didn't feel dizzy. I touched the cold terrazzo floor with my toes. Then I lay back down.

The next night, I sat up again. Then I stood. My body felt unnaturally heavy, like when you have been swimming all day and then climb onto dry land, but my knees didn't buckle. I walked slowly to the far side of the room, back again. My heart was pounding. I sat on the bed, stood, sat. It was almost daylight before I lay down again.

The last night before Dr. Barsamian came, I walked down the hall. The central air cut on, but otherwise the house was silent. Bertha and Gretel were asleep on their beds in my parents' room. I moved from the carpeted living room to the kitchen and opened the refrigerator. The light seemed dangerously bright, but still I stood there. I put my finger into a container of Cool Whip, but with my jaw wired shut there was no way to lick it off, to eat anything in the refrigerator. I couldn't even take a drink of water without a straw. I heard Lucky purring in his sleep, then the ice maker came on with a crash. I went back to bed.

The next day, when the time came for me to officially sit up, I said nothing about my rehearsals. My mother and father and Carol all watched as Dr. Barsamian helped me sit. "Whoa, now take it slow." Then I stood. Carol and my father applauded. I told them how weird it all felt, describing from memory how it had felt the other night. No one could understand much of what I was saying behind my wired teeth, but they smiled and I smiled. I looked happy, and I was, but underneath I thought this: that I was not just faking it now—I had been all along. There had never really been anything wrong with me, and this proved it. Or rather, what was really wrong with me had something to do with why I could never get my homework done, why I was always trying to think up some stupid story to get me out of whatever trouble I was in. Falling from that tree seemed like the biggest dodge of all, one that had really worked. I felt guilty and a little sick.

I got my jaw unwired, and I was now allowed to walk around the house and to go for short jaunts in a wheelchair around the neighborhood. My mother pushed me. It gave us both something to do. Twice a week, I got to ride in the car to Dr. Barsamian's office. I was so skinny that on the way to the doctor's my mother would stop at the local Bressler's 33 Flavors, where the owner would make me an ice-cream treat. He got into a competition with himself and each week made something larger and more exotic. We worked our way up to five flavors with six different toppings. He pinched my arm when I finished. "Almost ready for the oven," he joked if he thought I'd put on weight. "Not enough meat for soup," if I hadn't.

A week before the end of the school year, Miss Davis

came to see me. Off and on since I fell there had been some discussion about Miss Davis bringing by my schoolwork, about my making up what I'd missed, but now all that seemed forgotten. It seemed as if whatever my teachers had been teaching was not really important, as if all they had been doing was killing time. I really had gotten away with it. David Mize, though, failed and was being held back.

Somehow my mother and Miss Davis decided I was well enough to go to the end-of-the-year party, which was going to be a dance. I would have to go in the wheelchair, my mother said, afraid of rough boys who might knock me down.

Late that night, Carol came into my room. The PTA play was such a big success that she had just come from a command performance at the other elementary school in town. She was not wearing her silk ball gown, but her hair was still ratted on top of her head, and her cheeks were an unnatural red. "Hey, girl," she said, and perched on the side of my bed. I told her about the class dance, about how I had nothing to wear that fit over my brace. I told her I was afraid that no one would like me, that I didn't know how to remake the friends I had so recently made.

"Are you kidding?" Carol tapped my head lightly with one finger, as if she weren't Cinderella but my fairy godmother. "They're gonna love you."

WE ARRIVED EARLY, before the rest of the class, so I could get carried up the stairs and wheeled into place. I was not the only one at the dance in a wheelchair. Two other girls who had been out of school, Debbie Whitehead and Van Lewis, were back for the dance. They both had had rheumatic fever, something you got from having strep throat and your mother not being smart enough to take you to the doctor. At least this was what my mother's tone implied when she saw Debbie and Van. The fact that Debbie and Van's mothers were, oddly enough, the two scout leaders in town made my mother's disapproval complete. They, of all people, should have known better. My mother added me to the row of wheelchairs against the green wall of the multipurpose room and left, telling me she'd be back in an hour. Debbie was saying to Van, "You can't be on sulfa. That's not what they gave me."

The room was hung with streamers of black-and-white crêpe paper, clusters of white balloons. Mrs. Boggs, who was our homeroom mother, had made a cake decorated with thirty little black-and-white sugar diplomas, although you don't usually think of moving from fifth to sixth grade as graduating. She was taking cake decorating at my dad's junior college. She saw me, called out that she'd bring me a slice, but before she got a chance, the kids came pouring in, intent on punch and cake.

I was surprised at how familiar the faces were, even the pants, skirts, socks, shoes, which feet bounced, which dragged. I recognized the back of Ralph Katz's head from the hours I spent staring at it when we were seated in alphabetical order, in the same way Mark Lish got to stare at the back of mine. I saw Joanna Fosbleck and remembered the days we spent trying to build a Roman arch out of sugar cubes for our history project: the sugar cubes wouldn't stay stuck together, kept absorbing the glue, and then one night the ants got them. I saw Marly, my once and future best friend.

I knew that Carol was right, I could wheel myself over, right into the middle of the whole cake-hungry crowd, and it would be okay. People would knock on the front of my brace, want to roll the wheelchair as fast as they could.

But I didn't go, not just yet. I felt my wheelchair around me like my own private space capsule, my back brace a space suit inside that. Just for a moment more, I stayed where I was.

11

Before there were men in space, there were pets. Or at least animals. In kindergarten in D.C., our teacher had read to us about the brave chimpanzee Ham, Alan Shepard's predecessor, and about Enos, who flew just before John Glenn. Both chimps survived their Mercury flights.

In 1957, the year after I was born, the Russians sent the first of a long series of lap dogs into space. Poor Laika spent a dark, hungry, and lonely week in space with no way to return. No wonder *Laika* is Russian for *Barker*. Belka *(Squirrel)* and Strelka *(Little Arrow)* were luckier. They not only had each other for company aboard Sputnik 5 in August 1960, a year before Ham's flight, but also forty mice and two rats. Luckier still, they survived. Strelka went on to have a litter of six healthy puppies. Khrushchev sent one of

Even now, when I close my eyes and open the front door of our house in Cocoa and walk in memory out into our neighborhood, I think of the pets there, whose fates often echoed their families'. Luna Heights was basically a circle with a dozen low, one-story concrete block houses around the outside, four on the island in the middle, and only two roads in or out. One led into the older neighborhood of Indian Heights. The other street, next to our house, led down to the River Road.

Walking from our house around the circle, the first important pet was at the Mizes', next door. They had a collie named Arrow—I doubt she was named after Strelka—who followed David everywhere. She was sort of a neighborhood dog, our low-budget Lassie, who greeted the school bus every day. We recruited Arrow as the reindeer for our red wagon sled when we all went caroling one hot Florida Christmas. Later, when David had a paper route, she used to run in front of his bike, barking madly, waking everyone before their alarm clocks had a chance to go off.

Then one morning, running full tilt and looking back for David, Arrow flew into a telephone pole and broke her neck. It killed her instantly. At the time, it seemed an almost inconceivable tragedy. What would the neighborhood be without Arrow? Years later, when one of David's sisters was killed in a one-car accident on River Road, probably just doing the same thoughtless, crazy teenager things we all did, my first thought was of what had happened to Arrow.

Down from the Mizes were the Barnses, whose only child, Lori, was the girliest of girls, the one who never wanted to play with more than one of us at a time and never anywhere but at her house and never anything but Barbies. The Barnses owned a Chihuahua named Pepe who barked madly whenever I knocked on the door, throwing himself into the air in little jumping-bean frenzies, until invariably he'd stop and throw up on the carpet at my feet. Then Mrs. Barns would appear with a wad of paper towels and scold me. "Don't excite Pepe," she would say. As if there were any way not to.

Mrs. Barns and Lori seemed to spend all their time indoors with Pepe, drinking Cokes out of tall frosted glasses while painting their toenails and Pepe's matching colors, while Mr. Barns, in his never-ending quest for the perfect lawn, spent hours down on his knees trimming the stray blades around his palm trees with a pair of special patented grass scissors.

Then Mr. Barns went on a business trip to California and never came back, leaving his wife and Lori and Pepe to carry on without him. In a few months, his lawn turned from putting green to sand trap. I can't say Mrs. Barns or Lori looked as if they even noticed, but poor Pepe went into decline, barely hopping when anyone knocked. Before long he was buried under what was left of the lawn, in the loose, dry white sand.

I saw Arrow and Pepe when I went to see David or Lori, but I also knew the pets who didn't live with kids, like Sir Galahad Worthington, the world's oldest beagle, who lived with an elderly couple, the Worthingtons, on the far side of the circle. Sir Galahad was so old something had gone wrong with his hormones, making him smell like a female dog in heat. Mrs. Worthington had to walk him with a red, battery-powered cattle prod in one hand to shock any dogs who might get the wrong idea. Every afternoon they took a slow stroll—Mrs. Worthington smoked and had emphysema—down to the River Road entrance to the neighborhood where they waited until Mr. Worthington, returning from wherever he spent his days, stopped and picked them up in his big Lincoln Continental for a one-block air-conditioned ride home.

Sitting beside her one day as she waited, I had Mrs. Worthington tell me the story of how she'd gotten Sir Galahad. Years before, she said, she'd been a reporter in Chicago. Walking home one cold night, she had found Sir Galahad abandoned in an alley next to her newspaper's offices. Because he had a broken leg, she took him to a vet, who told her Sir Galahad was obviously an expensive, pedigreed beagle. As a reporter, it seemed odd to her that someone would dump a dog worth real money.

So she wrote an article about Sir Galahad, asking if any-one had lost a beagle puppy. It turned out that Sir Galahad's entire litter and his mother, a national champion, had been kidnapped from their breeder and held for ransom. The kid-nappers had gotten rid of Sir Galahad when they realized he was hurt. When the article was published, the other puppies and their mother were set free, found, and returned to the breeder. When she heard the news, Mrs. Worthington pre-pared to give up Sir Galahad, knowing she could never af-ford to buy such an expensive dog. But the breeder, grateful for her help, had said Sir Galahad, with his bad leg, would never make a show dog and had let the Worthingtons keep him.

When I thought of this story, I imagined Mrs. Worthing-ton as young and brave, a bit like Lois Lane on assignment from *The Daily Planet,* though if you grant Sir Galahad an ordinary span of dog life, Mrs. Worthington was probably at least fifty when the Great Dognaping happened. By the time I knew them, the Worthingtons and Sir Galahad seemed equally ancient, and even my mother wondered out loud who would take care of Sir Galahad and Mr. Worthington if anything happened to Mrs. Worthington. In the end, Sir Galahad died first, leaving Mrs. Worthington to take her slow walks alone.

Next to the Worthingtons lived the Stratoses, who had a

frighteningly large red parrot, Astro, the only pet in the neighborhood with a true space age name. The Stratoses often left Astro tied to the clothesline in the backyard. Most mornings when we neighborhood kids, Carol, Marly, David, and me, cut through the Stratoses' yard to get to the bus stop before school, Astro would have his head tucked under one crayon-red wing, as if deep in bird sleep. Four mornings out of five, he would stay that way. Then on the fifth, when we'd almost forgotten he was there, when we were walking along talking and paying him no attention at all, Astro would spread his wings, open his orange beak, and scream. Once Carol threw her algebra book in the air, scattering proofs everywhere. Once Marly's little brother started to hiccup, then to cry.

The Stratoses were the talk of the neighborhood while they lived there. They had made all their money selling Mink Oil Bath Beads in a pyramid scheme run by a man named Glen Turner who appeared on TV telling everyone to Dare to Be Great. They had moved into an empty house, painted it bright Athenian blue, and put two naked Greek statues in their front yard. They put a sign over the door saying WELCOME TO THE STRATOSPHERE and invited the neighbors over to let them in on the great Mink Oil deal.

Eventually Turner went to jail. The bank foreclosed on the mortgage on the Stratoses' house. They moved out in the middle of the night, taking with them not only their furniture and the statues, but the garage door, the toilets, the bathtubs, the water heater, the light fixtures, and even some of the wiring. These were things the bank thought it owned. Astro, though, they set free, and he joined several other parrots who'd escaped from jungle attractions and roadside zoos around the state.

Astro remembered where his home, or at least our neighborhood, was. Once, a woman driving through the neighborhood stopped and rang our doorbell to tell us our parrot had escaped and was sitting in an orange tree. I peered cautiously into the front yard. Astro glared back at me, no friendlier than ever. I told the woman we didn't have a bird and slammed the door before Astro could open his beak to scream at me.

The last time I saw him, I had opened the backdoor to take out some trash and found Astro and five large green parrots with orange beaks and feet sitting on the telephone wire looking down at me like so many vultures. I had just seen Hitchcock's *The Birds*. I dropped the trash and jumped back inside. We had a couple of cold winters after that, and I thought maybe the cold had gotten Astro. Years later, my father sent me a clipping about exotic birds taking over south Florida, driving out the indigenous species. I swear the bird in the illustration, perched high in an oleander somewhere near Miami, was Astro.

Looking back, I can't help feeling that Arrow's death foreshadowed David's sister's, the first tragedy preparing the way for the next. Or that Sir Galahad Worthington's death was clearly a sign of things to come for the human Worthingtons. Astro's fate was an example for everyone who came to Florida with high hopes and stayed even when they weren't necessarily welcome.

I was part of a family that raised dogs' status to the level of children's. (Remember my mother's *four-legged girls* and *two-legged girls*?) Snapshot for snapshot, there are more sleeping cats and dachshunds than people in any box of our family photos. We took turns hugging and kissing the pets instead of each other. We loved our pets. They loved us. We were a family.

Then one day, for no apparent reason, Bertha tried to kill Gretel. The trouble had started earlier, with growls and fierce looks that left Gretel shaking. This time, while the pets were on their morning walk, my mother holding their leashes, Bertha went for Gretel's throat. There was blood and howling and a trip to the vet. My parents decided the only thing to do was to give Gretel away. Bertha, though obviously in the wrong, would never adjust to a new family, they said. Gretel, on the other hand, who we had always joked would have happily gone home in a sack with any burglar, would do just fine. My father asked around and found a couple that taught at the college who agreed to take her.

I remember sitting at the kitchen table—Gretel at our feet, Bertha banished to the garage—and being told of my parent's decision. Carol started crying. Gretel was her favorite. I wanted to protest, but I didn't know what to say, how to put into words the magnitude of this violation. If our dogs were family and one hated the other, what did it say about us? If Gretel was my mother's four-legged daughter, what did it mean that she was willing to give her away in the name of harmony and practicality? Bertha had always been my favorite, but goofy and bowlegged Gretel was duck-footed and easygoing me in the family mythology. The dog me was being sent to join another family.

We went to visit Gretel in her new home just once. Carol and I had begged and begged, but my parents kept putting us off. Gretel needed time to get adjusted, they said. It wouldn't be fair to her new owners. Finally one Saturday, we did go. Her new owners lived in the same subdivision on Cocoa Beach where the Henrys had lived. Their house was pale yellow and on a canal. It could have been the same house Carol and I had run through on our second day in Florida.

Gretel seemed happy to see us, but not overly so. She rolled on her back and wagged her tail, but there was no accompanying spray of little wet drops of pee, the disgusting but true sign of dachshund enthusiasm. She ran out in the backyard with us while her new owners told cute stories about how sometimes they would come home to find the living room wrapped in long streamers of toilet paper or the kitchen dusted with pancake mix, and a powdered Gretel looking very innocent. This confirmed something I'd suspected before. When Bertha and Gretel had lived with us and anything like that happened, Bertha always looked the guiltiest and always got the blame.

After Gretel left, no one scattered Kotex around the living room or ate all the Dixie cups from the trash can in the bathroom. Bertha, it seemed, had not been the idea man. Perhaps it should have been obvious, but Bertha was so much in charge in every other way that my parents never suspected. It figured. Over the years, I had somehow talked Carol, my older, supposedly in-charge sister, into doing very crazy things. Once in Maryland, I'd persuaded her to slide down the laundry chute, even though we were on the third floor. I told her I had already done it, and it was great fun. Luckily, she got stuck almost right away. Even more luckily, I was able to lower a sheet to her so she could climb out. Neither of us told our parents about it.

One thing Gretel did should have given my parents some hint of her secretly adventurous nature. Just after we had moved to Cocoa, my mother found her in the backyard having some kind of seizure and rushed her to the vet. She'd licked a poisonous frog, the vet said. Dogs in Florida did that, but only once. After that they knew better. But not Gretel. Twice more my mother found her stiff on her back, her eyes wide open, as if she were on some kind of dachshund LSD, the trip worth the risk of the seizure. This was one illicit dog pleasure she was never able to convince Bertha to try. I wondered at the time if it meant that I, too, as the human Gretel, would one day think it worth risking life and limb for the sake of some great high.

The day of our visit, we left Gretel standing by the canal, barking at the fish, and we drove home saying it looked like she was happy, that she had a good home. We said we would come back, already knowing we wouldn't.

A year later, her owners called with sad news. They'd come home from work that day to find Gretel, with a frog in her mouth, drowned in the canal.

12 October 1968

Paul Maltezo was drowning and only I could save him.

Mrs. Henry was our swimming instructor. When Dr. Henry left town, she'd bought a smaller house with a bigger pool in the neighborhood next to ours and reopened her swimming school. Mrs. Henry had picked Paul to play the victim for my junior lifesaving test because she knew he couldn't say no. His sister, Lynn, was taking the test, too. Paul was fifteen, the ninth-grade class president of Clearlake Junior High School (the Rockets). He was tall and tanned, and he was a god. Lynn and I were both just twelve, only a month into the world of seventh grade and junior high.

Could you rescue a god? I had to try. I dove in and swam straight toward Paul, looking for an easy hold, but he was a panicky drowner. He had already passed senior lifesaving and knew exactly what I would try. He grabbed my hair and tried to pull me under. I jerked my head, leaving some blond hair in his hand, and tried again.

This time he kicked me hard right where I didn't have breasts to speak of yet. I sank, pretending he'd knocked the wind out of me. Then I dove deep and came up behind him, got him in a good cross-chest lock. I side-stroked the two of us toward the end of the pool. Paul wasn't done yet. He threw his legs high in the air, and we went under. When we came up, both of us were coughing.

I felt Mrs. Henry's eyes on me. She raised her stopwatch. I had maybe another minute, and we were only halfway to the shallow end. Paul rocked sideways, trying to break my hold. He was bigger and stronger, and I couldn't believe he was being so unfair. I dug my nails into his side, as deep and as hard as I could. "Christ!" he said. But he stopped squirming.

We made it to the concrete steps, and I half dragged, half carried him out of the pool. "Time, Jesse," Mrs. Henry called out. Her stopwatch clicked. "You just made it." She offered me her hand. "Congratulations."

"Thank you, Mrs. Henry," I said.

Standing in the grass by the side of the pool, Paul showed off the four red, curved dents my nails had left. Mrs. Henry touched her finger to his scarred brown side, her blond head bent over his. Now that she was divorced, she'd stopped asking everyone to call her Lucille. "My, my," she said and laughed. I stood with my legs wrapped tight around each other, trying to disappear.

To my surprise, Paul brushed the dripping hair out of his eyes and smiled at me, not Mrs. Henry. "Scarred for life," he said.

After Lynn passed her test, too, we walked back to the Maltezos' still in our suits, ready to celebrate. Paul had stayed behind to help Mrs. Henry put away the floats, but I hoped he might come soon. We stood in the garage dripping, reluctant to go in the house where our clothes were because the air-conditioning would freeze us. "Jeez," Lynn said, looking at my chest, "I think my dad's home. What if he sees you like that?"

I looked down. My nipples stood at attention, showing clearly through the fabric of my bathing suit. I crossed my arms tight across my chest, felt my face turn red. Lynn rolled her eyes, disgusted both with my breasts and with my embarrassment. She went over to a box in the corner of the garage. "Mom keeps some old clothes here for yard work," she said. "Take this." She handed me a madras plaid shirt. Inside the button-down collar was a name tag: PAUL MALTEZO. The shirt was soft and dry and warm, pure cotton too worn to hold a wrinkle.

"Thanks," I said and meant it.

The back door opened. "Are you girls coming in or not?" It was Mrs. Maltezo. She worked part-time as a nurse for my pediatrician, Dr. Blue, so I knew her better than some moms. "I put out some Tab and Bugles," she said, enticing us. We went in. The Maltezos had lived in Cocoa longer than anyone else I knew. Lynn had been born there. Even Mrs. Maltezo had been born in Florida—in Tampa, to a family that had made cigars. Their kitchen counter, now topped with a bowl of Bugles and two large, sweating tumblers of diet soda, was made out of a slab of marble. Marble upon which, Mrs. Maltezo said, girls working for her father used to roll the finest cigars to be had on the planet.

Just as we finished our snack, Mr. Maltezo came in. He had a half-bushel basket of oranges in his arms. "George Pickering sent them home with me," he said. He'd spent the morning in Kissimmee. Mr. Maltezo ran an insurance office in downtown Cocoa and traveled a lot on business and to things like University of Florida football games making contacts. He set the oranges on the marble counter and took the highball Mrs. Maltezo offered him. He smiled down at Lynn and me perched on our stools at the counter, our bare legs crossed.

"Don't you girls look nice," he said.

At school the next week, Lynn and I were in the back row in PE waving our arms and pretending to do jumping jacks, when she told me Paul wanted his shirt back.

"Why?" I said. I'd been wearing it around the house. I liked it. "It's just a rag."

"Yeah, but he's pissed. It was Dad's when he was in high school and so it means something to him."

I nodded. "Okay, tomorrow."

The next day I pretended to forget, but on Friday I had to give it back. That same day Paul was on an Orlando TV station's evening news and in the local paper the next morning. He and two friends from his science class were going into space. That is, they were going to lock themselves in the Maltezos' Airstream travel trailer and not leave it for as long as the upcoming Apollo 7 mission lasted. Apollo 7 was the first moon mission since Apollo 1 burned up on the pad. They had the principal's permission to miss school.

"Yeah," Lynn said when I asked her about it, "can you believe it? He'll miss almost two *weeks* of school. Too bad girls can't be astronauts." I nodded. A year ago, it had seemed impossibly unfair that women couldn't be astronauts, real astronauts. Now I was only bummed that it meant I couldn't blast off in the Maltezos' Airstream and spend ten days nearly alone in space with Paul.

She said she might not be getting out of any classes, but that her mother had promised she could have a slumber party on Friday, a week after the launch. She could invite up to ten girls, one for every day Apollo 7 was supposed to be in space. Paul and his friends would still be orbiting in the Maltezos' yard. I thought about Paul asleep inside his aluminum-skinned capsule just yards from where we would be making popcorn and pizza in the Maltezos' kitchen. If I couldn't be inside with him, at least I could be close. *Please God,* I thought as Lynn told me, *let me be one of the chosen.*

She invited me that afternoon on the bus and also asked Carol, which made it almost certain I could go. She asked Marly Boggs, too, whom she knew had been my best friend before her. Now that we were in junior high, Marly and I were never in a class together. I told myself I was busy with swimming and hardly saw her anymore. The truth was, coming off the bus on the first day at junior high school, we'd been so scared we'd held hands. Now, after one month in the big social swim of Clearlake Junior High, I found it mortifying to remember I'd been seen holding hands with a girl.

That next week all the talk in Cocoa was of Apollo 7. After what had happened to Apollo 1, the deaths of the three astronauts, everyone was nervous. Sure, the capsule had been completely redesigned. No more pure oxygen. New emergency procedures. Nothing unexpected could or would happen. But no one had foreseen the first tragedy either. Everyone thought the astronauts—Wally Schirra, Donn Eisele, and Walt Cunningham—were brave. No one envied their wives. This sense of bravery in the face of danger rubbed off on Paul and his friends. People had always thought he was special. Now in the rush between classes, they stepped off the sidewalk onto the grass to let him go by. Even the bad boys, the ones who spent all their time lounging in the hallways waiting to be paddled by the assistant principal, moved aside.

The papers, too, were full of Apollo features. The impending launch knocked the war in Vietnam and even the upcoming presidential election onto the back pages. I was beginning to think I was against the war, but my mother had always been a big Johnson fan, crying, "Oh, God. Oh, no!" the night he announced he wasn't going to run again.

One night, when both my father and Carol were out, my mother and I ate dinner on TV trays and watched Walter Cronkite together. My mother was on pills now, Valium, something that her doctor prescribed. She had gone to him worried she was getting Parkinson's disease like her mother, but he'd found no sign of that, no sign of anything you could put a name to.

I thought the pills made her worse, not better. She often spent the whole day in bed, getting up only to fix us something that passed for dinner, drifting around the kitchen opening cans, setting the table, not saying a word. When I'd told my father what I thought, he'd just said, "Dr. Bach says she'd be much worse without medication."

This night, my mother was unusually chatty. Like LBJ, she had her doubts about Humphrey. Johnson, she said, reminded her of her father, a good tyrant, a strong man. LBJ had had to be. He'd started out life a poor school-teacher just like she had. Look what he made of his life. Humphrey, on the other hand, was weak. Look at the way he let Johnson walk all over him. Humphrey was intelligent, no doubt about that, but in ways that didn't do him or any-body else much good. Like so many smart people, she'd added. Though she didn't say so, I knew she was talking about my father. Maybe about me, too.

In spite of my mother's misgivings, or because of them, I decided I was for Humphrey all the way, a radical decision at our junior high. Our school was getting ready to hold a mock election on the same day as the real thing, and George Wallace was going to win by a landslide. I had gotten my fa-ther to drive me to the Humphrey headquarters, a tiny store-front downtown by the library, where I paid fifty cents for an HHH button the size of a small dinner plate. I wore it on my purse. Twice during class change, someone took a look at my Humphrey button and tried to push me down the stairs. Lynn Maltezo and Marly Boggs were both staunchly for Nixon.

On Friday, the day of the launch, Paul and the other mock astronauts were home, loading their silver capsule, running a last check of supplies with Mrs. Maltezo. They had a chemical toilet; instructions from Mr. Donner, their science teacher, for a set of authentic space experiments; and a deck of cards in case they got bored. They had several cases of baby food, the closest they could come to what the astronauts ate. All the windows were covered with aluminum foil with tiny holes poked in it so the sunlight shining through would look like stars in the black night of space. All morning at school, I wished I were there, outside Paul's Airstream rocket. If I couldn't be an astronaut, I would be the perfect flight controller, handmaiden to the gods. Instead I had PE, then science, where we had been stuck on the reproduction of liverworts for some time. Then the principal came on the intercom and said we could all file out onto the driver's ed range to watch the launch.

At eleven A.M. Schirra and the others headed across the blue Florida sky trailing white smoke. The blast rattled the windows in the twenty portable classrooms, portable bathroom, and portable lunchroom it took to house and service all us extra space kids. No doubt it rattled the windows of the Airstream where Paul and his friends sat, strapped into lawn chairs rigged for the purpose. "We have liftoff," the controllers at the Cape said. "Blastoff," Mrs. Maltezo said into her walkie-talkie to Paul, waving to the boys though they couldn't see her. *Bon voyage.*

On Saturday afternoon, half the neighborhood gathered

in the Maltezos' yard. Mrs. Maltezo had set up refreshments on the picnic table. There were squares of the special Astronauts' Fruitcake she had baked for the boys to take into orbit. The recipe, clipped from the paper, was beside the plate: *This fruitcake identical to the ones the astronauts eat in Space,* it read, *has energy power a plenty for us earthlings who live in this globe's field of gravity.* I took a square and bit into it. It tasted just like the fruitcake my mother's brother in Texas sent us every year. Which is to say, it tasted awful. I spit out my first bite into my hand, then dropped the whole piece discreetly onto the lawn under the picnic table where I hoped some neighborhood dog would find it. About seven pieces were already there. So far, no dogs had been interested.

As I helped myself to a cupcake with a tiny American flag on a toothpick in it, Mrs. Maltezo came over and poured me a glass of Tang, drink of the astronauts. She asked me if I had heard the news.

"What news?" I asked

"The president called."

"Our president?" I almost dropped my orange drink.

Mrs. Maltezo nodded. "LBJ." She looked pleased, but I couldn't help thinking that my mother would have been more than pleased. She would have been speechless, awestruck, to speak to Johnson. If only I'd been the kind of kid who merited a call from the president.

Mrs. Maltezo went on. "First thing this morning. Woke us up. He saw the piece about the boys on Walter Cronkite and wanted to talk to Paul." And so he had, though only briefly. Paul, standing on principle, had refused to leave the Airstream to come to the phone. So Mr. Maltezo had to hold the walkie-talkie up to the receiver. The president was both pleased and proud. "A new generation is readying itself for space," President Johnson had told Mr. Maltezo, who had two Nixon signs stuck in his yard.

That night, the TV news was all about Wally Schirra, three-time space veteran, who had just come down with the first head cold in space. By Monday the excitement had died down at school. Paul wasn't there, and out of sight was out of mind. Instead, everyone was talking about the new order from the principal that all homeroom teachers measure girls' skirts to make sure they ended no more than ten inches above their knees. Any shorter, he announced, was a violation of the school's dress code. My homeroom teacher, who taught shop, didn't bother, but I could see girls across the hall lined up on their knees while Madame Muller, our French teacher, measured their bare legs with a yardstick. One of the teachers ripped the hems out of all but one of her girls' skirts, then sent them to the nurse's office to be sent home to change. The only girl who didn't flunk the ten-inch test belonged to a Pentecostal sect that wore ankle-length skirts and giant beehive hairdos on their heads. God had told them never to cut their hair.

I saw Carol at my locker after homeroom. She said, "Let them try that on me. Dad will call a lawyer."

"Yeah," I said, though I was less sure. Although I didn't have a ruler on me, I was pretty sure the hem of my dress, an orange-and-yellow flowered A-line, was at least twelve inches above my kneecaps.

The next day, the school paper ran an actual copy of the school dress code on the front page. Who knows where the kids who worked on the paper found it or how they managed to get to the mimeograph machine in the middle of the night to run off the extra edition or how they managed without Paul, who was editor of the paper. The official code (written in 1959) called for boys to wear white shirts with ties and girls to wear either shirtwaists in solid colors or white blouses and blue skirts. Socks and black shoes were required for both. On Fridays, everyone was to wear spirit beanies. The article turned the dress code into a joke. Even the principal had to admit it. Eventually a revised dress code would be issued that even allowed blue jeans. Flip-flops were banned as a health and safety hazard, but people wore them anyway. This whole revolution took place while Paul Maltezo, class president, was in orbit and unavailable.

By Thursday, when I stopped by the Maltezos' house in

my bathing suit to get Lynn for swimming lessons, the yard was empty except for the Airstream. Only the picnic table served as a reminder of Saturday's excitement. Lynn was slumped in a lawn chair, picking nail polish off her toenails and talking to Paul on the walkie-talkie.

"No," she was saying, "I don't see why I should run down the battery on my transistor radio just so you *boys* can hear music. If you're bored, go walk in space."

She rolled her eyes. "All they do is complain. The toilet smells. All of the baby food except the vanilla pudding tastes awful. The seeds for their experiment didn't sprout. They're bored." She sighed. "I'm bored. Here, you talk to them. I'm going inside and get my suit."

I pressed the button on the walkie-talkie. "Hey," I said, "Earth to Paul."

"Lynn?" Paul's voice crackled back.

Somehow it seemed easier to talk to him when I couldn't see him. "Jesse," I said, "you know, the girl who saved your life."

"Well, hello there, lifesaver." I asked him what he was doing, and he said they were playing poker for the last jars of pudding. After that, all that was left was strained peas and fruitcake.

"Can you see me?" I asked, looking at my reflection in the Airstream. The curve of aluminum skin made me look tall, languid, like a model by the side of some gorgeous blue magazine pool.

"No, not unless I peeked under the aluminum foil," Paul said, "and that would be cheating."

"You wouldn't cheat?"

"No," Paul said, "I wouldn't."

But one of the other boys was less scrupulous. I heard him say, "Hey, who's the skinny kid in the swimsuit? Your girl—" Then Paul released the button, cutting communications. My face turned bright red with embarrassment. *Who's the skinny kid?*

Lynn reappeared. She didn't seem to notice. "Come on," she said. "We're late."

We needn't have hurried though. We were supposed to be practicing our diving—I could never keep my feet together—but as soon as we got in the pool it started to thunder and lightning. Then it poured. "Out of the pool, girls," Mrs. Henry said, clapping her hands. We sat out the downpour on Mrs. Henry's long screened porch, which had a Ping-Pong table and big piles of magazines. In the summer the porch was filled with kids waiting for the next hour of lessons and parents waiting to take their young swimmers home. By October, most of the classes were over, only Lynn and I had stayed on to finish our lifesaving class and practice our diving. Mrs. Henry disappeared into the pump house beside the pool to do something with the filters. Lynn and I played a mad game of Ping-Pong, bouncing the ball off the low ceiling, the screens, the concrete block walls. Then we sat and flipped through fashion magazines, peeling apart pages stuck together by the humidity to peer at women with wide eyes, lashes sticky with black mascara, and chests almost as flat as ours.

In my house, we never had these kinds of magazines, only *Time, Reader's Digest,* and *National Geographic.* I suppose my mother thought women's magazines were foolish, full of unnecessary and frivolous advice. In some ways, I agreed. Surely there was more to life than the makeup and diet tips their covers promised when I saw them at the supermarket. But at least the magazines were willing to offer advice on what it took to be a woman. The year before, when my mother had noticed the little bust I'd managed to develop, she'd taken me to the lingerie department at Belk's for a fitting and turned me over to a very busty white-haired clerk with a measuring tape around her neck. Mom had announced, "This young lady needs a good-quality bra." Other than that, I'd been on my own.

Mrs. Maltezo arrived, pulling her Cadillac up close to the screened backdoor so Lynn could run out. She rolled down her window a crack and offered to give me a lift home, but I yelled back through the rain that my father was supposed to stop for me after picking up Carol from chorus practice. They drove off. I could have gone with them anyway. Carol, if not my father, would guess the lesson was rained out. Or Mrs. Henry would have told him. But I hated the idea of being in the house with only Bertha, Lucky, and my drugged mother. Now that Gretel was gone, the house reminded me of a creepy mansion in some movie where people start mysteriously disappearing one by one.

I picked up another magazine. *Ten Ways Men Like to Be Kissed!! Page 154!!* the cover read. I was trying to unstick page 154 from 155 when Mrs. Henry reappeared with two tall aluminum tumblers of iced tea. She set them on the Ping-Pong table, glancing at the magazine. She lit a mentholated cigarette. "What is it you need to know about kissing?" she said. She was wearing a white two-piece suit, and her skin was the deep, even brown of dark Karo syrup.

I thought about it. I needed to know everything. "How do you get a boy to kiss you?"

Mrs. Henry didn't laugh. She took a deep drag on her cigarette, giving the question serious thought. "Pretend I'm a boy. Stand up," she said. "Closer." She took my shoulders between two of her slender brown fingers and maneuvered me until my toes were touching hers. "First tilt your head back," she said, putting one finger under my chin and lifting it, "and wet your lips." I licked them nervously, once, twice.

"Now," Mrs. Henry said, breathing out a cloud of mentholated smoke, "close your eyes." Mrs. Henry lightly touched her lips to mine. I smelled suntan lotion and the chlorine in her hair. "There," she said, stepping back. "Easy as pie. Any boy would have to be crazy not to want to kiss you."

She handed me my glass of tea. I licked my lips. They tasted like Mrs. Henry.

IN THE END, Mrs. Henry drove me home. My father forgot—not that unusual—but for the first time ever, Carol forgot to remind him. By the time I got home, I was ready to be mad at her. I found her in the kitchen, standing at the refrigerator, pouring a glass of Hawaiian Punch. I slapped my rolled towel on the kitchen table. "Have you heard the news?" she asked me, not noticing that I was angry. "Jackie Kennedy is going to marry some old rich Greek guy. She's hidden away on his yacht in the Mediterranean." Carol made a face and drained the glass of sweet red punch as if washing a bitter taste from her mouth. "Isn't that disgusting? What would President Kennedy have said?" Carol had taken down her autographed color picture of JFK, but I knew she still had it, carefully stored in her sock and underwear drawer, along with the proof Kennedy half-dollars my mother had bought us when she worked at the Treasury. I understood why this news had made her forget about picking me up at Mrs. Henry's.

"I bet he's spinning in his grave," I said, imagining just that, JFK tossing and turning in his coffin under his flickering gas eternal flame, imagining his bride in another man's arms.

"Her new husband isn't even an *American,*" she said.

Carol said all the other girls in the chorus were outraged, too. And when we watched Cronkite after dinner, it was clear the whole world was waiting for the first glimpse of Jackie transmuted—like gold into lead, Cinderella into the Wicked Stepmother—into Mrs. Jacqueline Bouvier Kennedy Onassis. No one was thinking about poor Wally Schirra and his head cold circling the earth in Apollo 7 or about Paul asleep after a dinner of baby food and fruitcake in the Maltezos' dark backyard. No one, that is, except me.

That night I dreamed we were both in our bathing suits floating in the deep night of space. Paul was ahead of me, and I was trying to rescue him as I had in Mrs. Henry's pool. Though I could almost touch his warm, bare skin, he kept bobbing away.

13

On Friday, the eighth day in space for Apollo 7 and Paul and the day of Lynn's slumber party, Dawn Kartorski and I were carrying an archery target from the gym out to the far side of the field for PE. Halfway there, Dawn dropped her end. This was understandable. The targets were woven straw, about five feet across, heavy and awkward to carry. Unfortunately Pammy Derby was right behind me with a fistful of quivers, the spiked metal stands that, stuck in the ground, held the arrows for each shooter. When I stopped short, Pammy kept going and drove a quiver into the soft flesh behind my knee just below the hem of my navy blue gym suit. "Hey," I said, "watch it." It didn't really hurt. I pulled the quiver out. It left one moon-shaped crescent in my leg, like the marks my nails had left in Paul Maltezo's side but deeper. Blood oozed out.

Pammy took one look, dropped the quivers, and fainted. Dawn, who didn't realize what was happening, turned around and saw Pammy lying on the ground surrounded by metal quivers, her gym suit somehow unsnapped in the front to reveal a corner of white, lacy bra. For no reason I could see, Dawn screamed. That brought Miss Jepson, the PE teacher, running. "Give her air," she said, though the four of us were alone on the field. She crouched down and patted Pammy's face briskly. When Pammy sat woozily upright, Miss Jepson instructed Dawn to leave the target where she'd dropped it and help Pammy to the nurse's office. "Take it slow," she called to them as they started across the field, one leaning on the other.

"Miss J.," I said tentatively. Miss Jepson was tall and blond, with thin, ropy muscles in her legs and arms. She was the girl's dean as well as the PE teacher and the one who got to paddle the occasional girl sent to the office for that punishment usually reserved for boys. She knew I was a klutz, one of those girls who only passed PE because they always dressed out and showered. I tried to stay out of her way.

"What?" Miss Jepson snapped, swiveling to face me and seeing my leg for the first time. Blood was trickling slowly down the back of my leg, turning my sock a nice bright red.

"Holy moly," Miss J. said. "How did you get shot? We haven't even strung the bows yet."

"I didn't," I said. "I got stabbed by a quiver." I pointed to the sharpened metal stands lying scattered in the grass.

Miss Jepson shook her head, as if it were beyond her comprehension how a simple assignment to set up equipment could have turned into such wholesale slaughter. "Well, you'd better get to the nurse, too." I nodded and limped off the field.

Most days I would gladly have stabbed myself to get out of PE—that year I had achieved the lowest score a living human could make on the President's Physical Fitness test— but this time I was afraid I'd miss Lynn's slumber party if I was really hurt. When I opened the door to the office lobby, I saw Pammy stretched out on the couch with both the nurse and the principal's secretary tending to her. I guess she'd fainted again just trying to tell them what happened. "Excuse me," I said.

The secretary turned around, her mouth pursed in a frown. "Can't you see we're busy . . ." she began. Then she saw the blood soaking into the carpet.

"I was in archery class and . . ." I started.

"Oh, my God," the secretary said. "She's been *shot!*"

"Shot?" the nurse repeated, shifting her attention to me.

The principal, dark, balding Mr. Trumbell, who looked uncannily like the late Gus Grissom, popped out of his office. "Someone's been shot?"

"In archery class," the secretary said.

"By another student?" the principal asked, fully concerned now.

"By me," Pammy cried out from the couch, "by me," and burst into tears.

"It wasn't an arrow," I tried to explain, "and it wasn't her fault. It was a quiver. I was stabbed by a quiver." They all stood for a second, just staring at me. Then the nurse acted.

"Call her mother." She glanced at the girl sobbing on the couch. "Call both their mothers."

MY MOTHER ARRIVED, fully dressed, even wearing lipstick. Accidents had a way of getting her attention. She took me to see Dr. Blue. He was semiretired and only worked mornings, but luckily I'd been stabbed in first period. Mrs. Maltezo was there, so she cleaned the cut and my leg. "Tetanus booster and a gauze bandage," she said to me. "Too clean and small a puncture to stitch. Not too bad, but you are going to have yourself a cute little scar." Mrs. Maltezo smiled at my mother, who was sitting on a chair in the corner of the examining room, her head tilted back, her eyes closed, as if the sight of my blood had made her queasy. Actually, she was asleep. Dr. Blue stuck his handsome silver head in the examining room just long enough to agree with Mrs. Maltezo's diagnosis.

"You've got to watch out for Cupid and his arrows, young lady," he said and left laughing at his own joke.

After Mrs. Maltezo taped the bandage over the hole and wrapped a few rounds of gauze around my leg just to make sure the dressing stayed in place, I asked her, as both nurse and hostess, if I could still go to Lynn's slumber party. I figured she would say yes, and I wanted to stop my mother or Carol from getting any ideas about my not being well enough. Mrs. Maltezo smiled at my mother again. "It's all right with me," she said, "if it's all right with you, Mary."

My mother's eyes snapped open at the sound of her name. She sat up, running a hand over her hair, as if Mrs. Maltezo's blond perfect perm reminded her of how flat and gray hers was.

"Mrs. Maltezo says it's okay for me to come to Lynn's slumber party tonight, if it's okay with you, Mom," I said.

My mother snapped open her purse, looking for something, her cigarettes or maybe her car keys. "If she won't be a bother . . ." she said.

Mrs. Maltezo shook her head. "Jesse's never a bother." She turned her smile on me. "I'll check your dressing tonight before you girls go to sleep."

As if anyone ever slept at a slumber party.

• • •

WHEN MRS. BOGGS dropped Marly and Carol and me off at the Maltezos' it was still light, the red and purple of the sunset glinting off the silver back of the Airstream in the yard. My war wound made me a celebrity, and I got to tell my story, complete with imitations of both Miss J. and the principal, over and over, as each group of girls arrived. None of us went outside to talk to Paul or the other boys on the walkie-talkie. Though I'd been wanting to do that all day, ignoring Paul somehow felt better. Let him swing alone through the darkness of space, I thought as we spread out the pizza dough from the Chef Boyardee mixes, dribbled them with the bright red canned sauce and grainy canned cheese. As Carol, who'd been supervising, was about to stick the first one in the oven, Mrs. Maltezo said, "Wait." She'd bought pepperoni, to make it more like real Italian pizza. We watched as she added the slices, dealing them out like a deck of round cards.

While we were busy in the kitchen, Lynn took pictures of us with her father's old Polaroid Land camera. This was no simple white plastic Swinger, but a huge contraption with bellows and a bulb flash that was almost too heavy for Lynn to lift. The pictures, when they came out, were small and square. Lynn gave each shot exactly one minute to develop, then peeled back the sticky cover sheet, and there we were in black and white. Flour on our noses and hands deep in the dough. Dancing around with the little cans of cheese. The pictures curled into tight cylinders almost immediately, and you couldn't touch them or they would stick to your fingers. After she had shot the whole roll, Lynn rubbed each picture with some special milky solution that came in its own applicator the size of one of my mother's red lipsticks. "That keeps them from fading," she said. "In the morning, everyone can take one home."

We ate the pizzas, which were great—soft and greasy and terrifically salty. Carol picked all the pepperoni off hers and gave them to me. "Too hot," she said. The sausage slices made my mouth burn, but I ate them, washing them down with about a gallon of Coke.

"Man," Lynn said. "I bet we're going to have nightmares."

"Not if we stay up all night," I said.

After that, we changed into our PJs and watched *Theater X*, the late-night movie show the high school kids all watched. Some astronauts landed on a moon of Jupiter and discovered alien life in the form of a bunch of lonely young women in high heels. It was called *Fire Maidens of Outer Space*. The dance numbers were especially good.

When the movie was over at midnight, Carol announced she was going to Lynn's bedroom to sleep. "If anyone," she looked right at me, "wakes me up, I will personally kill them." Janie, the baby of the group, and three other girls decided they would try to sleep on the shag carpet in the family room. They headed off, trailing blankets and pillows.

After they were gone, Lynn said to the five of us left, "Hey, wanna see another movie?"

"How?" I said. After *Theater X,* the station had played the national anthem while the flag bravely waved and jets boomed through the sky. By midnight, all three Orlando channels were nothing but test patterns.

"Come on," Lynn said, waving for us to follow. We went down in the basement. The Maltezos' house was on a high bluff a block from the Indian River and had the only basement in Cocoa, maybe in the whole county. Her father, she said, had to bring in a crew from Georgia because no one in town knew how to dig one. "They said we'd hit water and have a swimming pool instead."

The basement was a little musty-smelling but seemed dry enough. There was a pool table and a bar and all sorts of those bar things grown-ups found funny, like Texas-size jiggers and a clock that said NO DRINKING BEFORE FIVE when all the numbers on the face were fives. The floor was made of linoleum squares that looked like playing cards. In the middle of the room, the King of Spades winked at the Queen of Hearts. Deep wooden storage closets were built into the wall along one end of the room. Lynn disappeared into one and came out with first a film projector and then a screen, which she set up in front of the bar. We sat on the linoleum floor, looked up at the show. There was no sound except for the projector's rattle. First we watched an old black-and-white Porky Pig cartoon of animals skating around noiselessly at the South Pole and defeating a hunter. Then a home movie in color of what I thought was Lynn as a baby playing on the beach with a much younger Mrs. Maltezo, who waved wildly for the camera.

"You were kind of a fat baby," Marly said, as we watched Mr. Maltezo's shadow move back and forth across the beach blanket where the baby lay, its mouth stretched wide in a silent wail.

"That's not *me*," Lynn answered, sounding disgusted. "I wasn't even born yet. That's Paulie."

I looked more closely. Paul *was* fat. And he looked deeply unhappy. Would our children, if we had children, look like that? In the movie, a disembodied hand waved a starfish in front of the baby. Paul only cried harder. I felt a sudden surge of maternal tenderness. I wanted to pick him up, make him stop crying, rock him to sleep and into a happier future. The basement seemed stuffy. I wanted to be outside. I wanted to talk to Paul on the walkie-talkie. Besides, linoleum playing cards made a hard theater seat. My quiver wound ached. I stretched my legs, started to stand up. The other girls shifted restlessly, too.

"Wait," Lynn said. "There's another movie." Something in the tone of her voice kept us where we were.

She said it was a film her father had brought back from a leave he'd had in Japan when he was in the army stationed in Korea. Something about the way Lynn had to dig in the very back of the closet told me it was a dirty movie, something we weren't supposed to see, though I couldn't have said how I knew about such things. It was in black and white and began with a shot of a Japanese tea house, a garden with a tiny bridge in the front. A girl in a kimono appeared at the door of the house. She walked gracefully toward the camera. When she was almost on the little bridge, she let her kimono slide to the ground. She smiled and nodded her dark lacquered head and stood there stark naked. Her breasts were nearly flat, no bigger than my tiny teacups, and she had no pubic hair. As she glided over the bridge and out of the frame, her naked twin appeared at the door of the house she had just left.

"This is stupid," Marly said, and got up and left. I could tell she didn't think much of my new friends. The rest of us stayed as the film cut to two girls—perhaps the same two, it was hard to tell—naked in a large wooden tub filled with steaming hot water. One waved a bath brush, the other one covered her mouth and giggled. I was puzzled. Except for their elaborate hair, these geishas looked like the rest of us in the showers in Miss Jepson's locker room. They didn't seem sexy to me, and what they did wasn't especially unusual or obscene. I didn't get it.

The movie was only a few minutes long. The projector clattered as the film ran out and flapped wildly. Lynn shut it off and turned on the lights. Nobody moved. Everyone seemed puzzled but oddly excited. One girl asked Lynn if we could see her dad's movie again. Lynn shook her head. "No, it might break," she said. "I have to put it back." Someone protested, "What difference would one more time make?" But Lynn was adamant. To distract us while she put everything away, she handed us a box of chocolates. Each one was wrapped in foil and shaped like a tiny liquor bottle. "Watch out," Lynn warned. "They've got real booze in them."

I unwrapped mine, which was marked Cream Sherry, and bit off the top. The liquid inside tasted anything but creamy. It burned my throat like cough syrup. I coughed, then ate the rest of the chocolate bottle, which wasn't half bad. I ate two more, Jamaican Rum and Crème de Menthe. The last one tasted a lot like Crest toothpaste.

"Won't your parents wonder what happened to these?" I asked Lynn. The four of us had all had at least two apiece, and the box, which had been full, was now nearly empty.

Lynn shrugged. "If she asks, I'll tell her Paul ate 'em."

When we climbed out of the basement, it seemed very,

very late. I had sworn I wasn't going to sleep at all, but now it seemed like a good idea to at least lie down for a while. I headed for the family room with its deep green-and-orange shag. Janie was asleep on the floor, and Marly and another girl snored gently on the facing couches. Lynn came in and found a place near the fireplace. Even she had given in to the idea of sleeping or at least resting for a while. I closed my eyes. *Just for a minute,* I told myself. The house was quiet except for the breathing of eleven girls, asleep or nearly so, and somewhere two parents, hopefully sound asleep, too.

The next thing I knew, I was dreaming that I was draped like a pepperoni on top of a giant pizza. An equally giant set of teeth were eating their way down the slice toward my greasy naked body. I screamed and sat up, my heart racing, my pajamas drenched in fresh sweat. Lynn was there. "If you're awake," she said, taking me by the hand, pulling me to my feet, "then come on. I've got a great idea."

She dragged me into the kitchen. A nearly whole pizza was left on the marble counter. She handed it to me. "No, please," I said. "I couldn't eat another bite."

Lynn shook her head, "It's not for you." She grabbed a couple of bottles of Coke from the refrigerator and tucked them under one arm. Then she grabbed the big Polaroid camera.

We went out in the yard. The grass was cool and damp

under my bare feet. It was quiet except for the tree frogs and very dark. The moon was nowhere to be seen, but the neighbor's yard lights were still on. Lynn set the Cokes on the picnic table and motioned for me to do the same with the pizza. Then she sat down on the table, too, her legs crossed. "Boy," she said in an unnaturally loud voice, loud enough to wake the neighbors, certainly loud enough to wake Paul. "There's nothing like a midnight snack of pepperoni pizza and Coke. I'm glad we came out here to eat it, but now I am soooo full and soooo tired." She faked a yawn so big I caught the silvery glint of one of her molars. "Let's go back to bed," she said. "Just leave that old pizza for the squirrels. I couldn't eat another bite."

We left the picnic table and crouched behind Mrs. Maltezo's Cadillac, Lynn holding the Polaroid at ready as if she were one of the reporters stalking Jackie Kennedy in Greece. The frogs sang. The palm trees in the front yard rustled dryly. Reflections from the neighbor's lights glistened on the pepperoni, and the cheese glowed with a light of its own. I could see the Cokes sweating. Then I heard a click like the sound of a small mousetrap snapping shut. Someone had popped the latch on the Airstream's door.

Roger London came out first. Tall and bony, he unfolded himself from the trailer with the awkward angularity of a praying mantis. I hoped it hadn't been Roger who called me skinny. Next came a boy whose name I could never remember. He was very short, shorter than me, and had a reputation as both a good surfer and the senior class clown. Roger's head swiveled on his shoulders, checking things out, making him look more than ever like some kind of bug. "It's all clear," he called over his shoulder into the trailer. Roger and the clown had already reached the picnic table and the pizza by the time Paul appeared at the trailer door. He stood there, eyes wide, his frown reminding me of the worried baby face I had just seen in the Maltezos' home movie. He looked awfully cute.

"I don't know," he said.

"Oh come on, Boy Astronaut," the little class clown said, with a nasal voice I recognized from the walkie-talkie. *He* was the one who'd made fun of the way I looked. "Step out on the surface of the moon for a little pizza." Then Paul stepped out of the trailer, but he didn't head for the pizza the way the other two boys had. He stared at the bushes that lined the driveway, stretched, and strolled toward the oleanders, as if they were what he had missed most in space.

"Better hurry up," Roger said, his mouth full of pizza. "We're not saving you any."

"Give me a minute," Paul said. He had reached the oleanders.

Lynn made a sound with her tongue like a chicken's cluck.

When she was taking a math test, this sound always meant she had come up with the answer. "Perfecto mundo," she said under her breath. In a split second she was up and aiming her camera.

When the flashbulb exploded, it became clear what Paul was doing. I saw his penis sticking out of his fly, slim and beautiful as any rocket, a long golden stream watering the oleander. "What!" I heard Roger say, frozen with a piece of pizza halfway to his mouth. "Crap," I heard the other boy, Mr. Funny Man, say.

Paul turned toward the flash, though he must have been nearly blind from the sudden burst of light, and said in a low, clear voice, "Lynn Megan Maltezo. You are dead meat."

Lynn tore the picture out of the camera, thrust it into my astonished hand. "Run," she said to me. "Don't let him get it."

I heard a low growl coming from Paul's direction, and I took off down the drive and into the street. I heard footsteps on the asphalt behind me. The pavement was rough, but I had callouses on my feet thick enough to stand a slow walk over live coals. I hadn't been running barefoot all those years for nothing. I kept going, heading downhill for the Indian River. My feet flew, and in the dark my strides were as long and fluid as they would have been on the moon. I felt the scab on the back of my leg break open, my quiver wound start to bleed a little, but I didn't care. I was flying. If I jumped high enough, I could escape gravity altogether and go tumbling through space. I held tight to the picture. After I crossed the River Road and reached the overgrown bank, I looked back. Paul was following me. The other boys had either ducked back into the trailer or were chasing Lynn. Paul was running so fast he seemed to be flying, too.

I scrambled through bushes, down the bank, and out onto the Maltezos' dock. It had been built back in the twenties when docks ran way out into the river and people put summer houses at the ends where they could sit safe from the mosquitoes and enjoy whatever breeze came up the river. A hurricane a few years before had taken the remnants of this dock's summer house away, but it was still a long dock, though not one in good repair. I didn't care. I ran down it full tilt, my feet hammering the rickety wood planking.

"Jesse," Paul called to me from the bank. "Watch out."

"Coward," I called back over my shoulder, slowing down a little as I picked my way over the missing boards.

Paul hit the dock fast. He knew where the rotten spots were and was gaining on me. I concentrated on my feet. *Careful. Keep going. Careful.* It was even darker on the river than it had been in the Maltezos' front yard. Then I was at the end of the dock. "Give me the picture, Jes," Paul said. He was right behind me. I jumped.

For an instant, I was floating, like somehow I was suddenly in space. Then my feet touched the water and immediately after, the slimy mud of the river's bottom. The water at the end of the dock was only up to my thighs. Ripe, sulfurous bubbles rose on all sides of me. I could feel the muck soaking into my pajamas, the bandage on the back of my leg. I'd be lucky if I didn't get blood poisoning, but I still had the picture. I tucked it into the back waistband of my pajamas.

Paul collapsed on his stomach on the end of the dock. "Phew," he said, smelling the sulfur. He was panting, out of shape after his week in space. "Give me that damn picture," he said, breathing hard. I was just beyond his reach, unless he wanted to come wading, too.

I shook my head. "I dropped it," I said.

Paul looked at me. "You *really* don't have it?"

I held up my empty hands. Paul looked at me and sighed. "You're crazy, you know that?"

I nodded. I was the one standing thigh-deep in the river, so I must be crazy. I wasn't, however, the one who'd just spent eight days in a sweaty, stinky trailer with two nasty boys and was about to lock myself in for three more. "Here," he said, offering me his hand. I put one mucky foot on the end of the dock for a leg up, and he stood and pulled, and somehow, not too gracefully, I managed to climb out of the river. Then we walked hand in hand, very carefully, back down the broken dock to the bank, water dripping from my PJs.

When we got to dry land, I tilted my head back and licked my lips twice. Paul kissed me, like he couldn't help it. He tasted like Astronaut Fruit Cake. No doubt I tasted like pepperoni pizza.

"Jesse?" It was Lynn, on the road above us. Paul froze. "Is that you? Have you got the picture?"

I did. I could feel it inside the waistband of my PJs, the elastic making it cut ever so slightly into the small of my back. I wanted to keep it. "No," I said, "I dropped it."

"Damn it," she said. I could see her face now, a white blob peering down from high on the bank. "Is that Paul? Hold on to him. I've got the camera."

Paul took off running down the sandy edge of the river, then up the neighbor's wooden steps to the road. By the time I got back to the Maltezos' house, all three boys were back in the Airstream, the pizza and the Cokes were gone, and a thin sliver of moon was beginning to rise.

I KEPT THE photograph, but I never peeled it apart. When I got home the next morning, it had been developing far longer than one minute. Anyway, I didn't have the special tube of fixative. I couldn't bear the idea that sweet, naked Paul would just fade away in the light of day. So I stuck it in the corner of my underwear drawer, where it remained until several years later, when my mother made me clean out my dresser. Then I found it stuck to the wood at the bottom of the drawer, fused into a puddle of its own gray chemicals.

After ninth grade, Paul transferred to a prep school. I saw him only twice in passing after that, once waterskiing on the river with friends in the summer and the last time coming out of a movie with a girl who looked a lot like Goldie Hawn on *Laugh-In*. But the square stain the Polaroid left in my dresser drawer never went away. It's still there. I saw it this morning when I was hunting for a matching pair of socks.

14 July 1969

When Apollo 11 blasted off for the moon with Neil Armstrong on board, I was 150 miles away at Turtle Lake Girl Scout Camp in the middle of the Ocala National Forest. In fact, I was practicing a water ballet to the sound of the "Theme from Love Story" blaring from a portable record player over the lake through a set of loudspeakers usually used for ordering campers out of the water in the case of a quick-moving Florida thunderstorm. I was in Aquatics, the unit at the camp that did the most swimming and boating, but even for us, water ballet was a bit of a stretch. This was the brainstorm of my tentmate, Celia, who had seen water ballet on TV during the Mexico City Olympics. Celia had just moved to Florida from California and was full of ideas.

Water ballet was not turning out to be one of her best ones. For one thing, the dark water of Turtle Lake, stained brown with tannin from the pine and cypress trees, made it impossible to see any fancy tricks done underwater. This limited our choreography to waving our hands and feet rhythmically in the air while we swam, but Celia had conned me and our other tentmate, Andrea, whom we called Andy, into participating anyway. Celia was a born leader.

We had just started the opening of our routine, the part where we swam in a circle doing the crawl while rhythmically dipping our hands in the water to the words, "How do I begin"—*dip, breathe, kick*—"to tell the story"—*dip, breathe, kick*—"of how great a love can be?"—*double dip, breathe, flip onto back*. Just as I was rolling over to start my backstroke, I noticed the water was full of tiny ripples, as if Turtle Lake were a glass in some nervous drinker's hand. On the shore, Happy, our counselor (named by the camp director after one of Snow White's dwarfs), lifted the tonearm from the record, and in place of the distorted music, I heard a familiar low rumble. Only a Saturn V rocket sounded like that. Apollo 11 was go. There were Americans on their way to walk on the moon.

Floating on my back, I shaded my eyes and looked up, expecting to see the white trail as the rocket headed downrange, but the sky was empty. We were too far north to see the launch, even though we could hear it. I stood up in the shoulder-deep water. Andy stood, too. I could hear cheers from the softball field, where most of the campers had gone after breakfast to watch the counselors play against a team from the YWCA camp, but I couldn't tell if they were cheering the launch or some spectacular slide into home. Celia, busy counting her strokes, bumped into me. "Hey, Doc," she said, calling me by the nickname she'd given me, based, she said, on how much I knew and not on the Disney dwarf of the same name. She stood, too. "Hey," she said, taking plugs out of her ears. "What happened to the music?" I started to tell her, but at the same moment Happy dropped the tone-arm on the record player, starting the music again with an awful sliding scratch that drowned me out.

After we finished our practice, Celia, Andy, and I sat on the floating dock, drying off. Even at ten in the morning, the sun was fiercely hot. I spent the whole summer burning, peeling, and burning again, too fair, really, to live under the Florida sun. No amount of Coppertone helped, so I had given up trying to do anything about it. Andy was also blond, but she had long tanned legs and arms—she was the tallest girl in the camp by a good six inches—and only seemed to burn on her nose and under her eyes, which she kept coated with zinc oxide. Even Celia, who was black, was light-skinned enough to have picked up a crop of freckles on her nose.

Celia was talking about how many miles of parking Disney World was going to have when it was finished, acres of asphalt for employees and tourists alike. You would have to take special trams, she said, just to get to the ticket window. She would know. Her father was one of the engineers trying to raise the huge new theme park out of the vast track of swamp and cattle land that Disney had secretly and carefully acquired outside Orlando over the years. Walt Disney had appeared one night on TV three years before and announced his plans for not only a theme park that would dwarf Disneyland, but a kind of space age city, Experimental Prototype Community of Tomorrow (EPCOT), where all the employees would live. Then Walt had died, leaving most of the kids on my bus more stricken after all those years of watching him introduce *The Wonderful World of Color* than they were when they heard that Bobbie Kennedy had been shot. Now Disney World was going to be all theme park, with the utopian village shelved indefinitely. Still, according to Celia, it was going to be a truly otherworldly place.

Andy was less keen on the idea. Her father had told her Disney was going to ruin the environment, a word I hadn't heard until Andy used it. Andy's father had a Ph.D. in philosophy but drove a Charles Chips truck, delivering potato chips and cookies around Casa Dega, a small spiritualist settlement near Orlando that had been founded way back in the twenties. Andy said Casa Dega was a place where you could get your fortune told by someone who looked just like your grandmother. You could also go to the spiritualist church, where the minister might call out something that fit only you, like, *I see there is a girl here whose father is a junior college administrator.* Andy had the distinction of having been the only Girl Scout brave enough to sell cookies in Casa Dega and so had won the statewide pennant for the most boxes sold. "Even at seances," she said, "sweet little old ladies always serve cookies. I just told them about how well they freeze. You know, so they could have them on hand all year."

As we sat sunning on the dock, Sneezy, one of the swimming instructors, came down to the swimming area with a couple of Red Caps. We all wore bathing caps coded to our swimming abilities to help the lifeguards spot someone who was in over her depth and thus in trouble. Celia and I were White Caps, junior lifesavers. Carol, who was at camp, too, was a White Cap. Andy, who hadn't taken her lifesaving test yet, was a Blue Cap, an advanced swimmer. Green Caps were intermediates. You had to be at least a Green to go out in the canoes or sailboats. Even Marly Boggs, who was at camp that summer and who was in Masquerade, the unit that mostly put on plays, was a Green Cap. Yellows were beginners, and that was bad enough. They weren't allowed to swim past the roped-in area at the end of the dock and weren't allowed in the boats. But Red Caps were the lowest of the low, the absolute nonswimmers. They weren't allowed near the lake without a counselor certified as both a senior lifesaver and a water safety instructor, in case they needed mouth-to-mouth.

This was the second of three two-week sessions that summer, and Carol and I were signed up for all three. The first session there had been no Red Caps at all, but this one there were two, both black girls from Tampa whom the Girl Scout Council had recruited as scholarship students. One girl, Leemona, was very dark and muscular and looked like she would be great in the stern of a canoe if she ever learned to swim enough to get her Green Cap. The other one, Charlotte, wore the thickest glasses I'd seen on a human being and always looked at the ground when she was walking, like she didn't trust it to be there. Charlotte, though, had a beautiful smile. She'd smiled at me the morning she arrived when I told her where to stand during the flag-raising ceremony and again when, as a waiter at breakfast, I passed a bowl of oatmeal to her and one to Leemona. Leemona, though, had looked daggers at me and at the oatmeal, like she couldn't think of anyone or any food in the whole world she hated more. About oatmeal, at least, she had my wholehearted agreement.

As soon as Celia saw Leemona and Charlotte with Sneezy, she frowned. Up until the two girls from Tampa arrived, Celia had been the only black girl at camp that summer. For some reason I couldn't understand, her reaction to the two new girls had been immediate and evident dislike—a feeling that Leemona, at least, returned. Now Celia stood up. Sneezy was trying to coax her two charges into the warm, shallow water, but Charlotte was clearly scared and Leemona was ignoring her, glaring instead at Celia. Both Leemona and Charlotte had on identical light blue two-piece bathing suits that clearly had never been in Turtle Lake, whose water instantly stained any color suit a deep iced-tea brown. Charlotte's suit was too big for her, and Leemona's was tight across her chest, as if they'd been bought for them by someone, maybe someone at the Girl Scout Council, who had never met them.

"Let's give the babies some room," Celia said, loud enough for them to hear. She walked down the dock to the shore swinging her hips as if she were on the runway in the Miss America contest. Andy rolled her eyes, but we both followed.

As we passed, I said to Charlotte, "Don't be scared. The water's as warm as a bathtub." Charlotte looked at the ground, as if she was either too scared to smile or had been warned by Leemona not to.

We trailed up from the lake, heading for the canteen. I wanted a roll of Clorets, which were rumored to discourage mosquitoes because the chlorophyll in them fooled the insects into thinking you were a bloodless plant. Besides, Clorets were as close as the canteen came to candy.

When we went in, Carol was standing by the window reading a letter. There was a hierarchy to units as well as bathing caps at the camp. General Registration, where Leemona and Charlotte were tentmates, was for the youngest, least-experienced campers. By breaking my back and missing my first summer at camp, I'd actually missed ever serving a stint there. A step up, though in my opinion, not a very high step, was Masquerade, where Marly Boggs was. Masqueraders put on shows for the rest of the camp in the big wooden theater left over from when Turtle Lake had been a WPA camp. Marly had told me that they were going to stage an old-fashioned melodrama and that she was cast as the villain, complete with black moustache and cape. Then, above Masquerade, came Campcraft, where I had spent my first summer in camp the year before, and then Aquatics, where I was now. Above them all was Outpost, whose campers lived on the other side of the lake in pup tents and only canoed across for supplies. Carol was in Outpost. Standing by the open window, bent over her mail, she looked to me like some fierce Indian maiden, if any Indian maidens had straight, long blond hair and wore the green shorts and white shirt of the Girl Scout camp uniform.

Carol's shorts were skintight, the coveted sign of a camper who'd been back summer after summer, and her shirt was covered with pins and patches. She was a determined camper and a serious scout. I loved camp, too, that's why I'd talked my parents into signing me up for all three sessions that summer. Other kids got homesick at camp. I used to joke that when I was home I got campsick. Carol loved all scouting—she was even talking about becoming a lifer, a professional Girl Scout like the camp director—but I found regular scout meetings during the year unbelievably boring. Carol saw me come in and waved me over. "Letter from Dad," she said, and handed me what she'd been reading.

My father had taken over writing us that summer; my mother had not sent a word. When Mrs. Boggs had driven Marly and me back to Cocoa for one night between sessions so we could get our clothes washed, my mother had barely seemed aware I'd been away. Dad always sent a letter a week, addressed to both Carol and me, that was mostly clippings from the newspaper. He sent our favorite comics— *Pogo* for me, *Peanuts* for Carol—and news he found interesting. The clippings this time were all about Ralph Abernathy and the poor people's march on the Cape. Rev-

erend Abernathy wanted Americans to remember there were
more pressing demands on the federal budget than sending
three men on a lunar vacation. I skimmed the article. I
wasn't sure why my father had sent it. Because he approved
of the march? Or just because it was local news, something
that was bound to be an impediment to tourism since it
would have tied up traffic at this morning's launch.

"Abernathy's the next Martin Luther King," Carol said, as
if she were crowning him herself. "But he's wrong about the
space program." She shook her head, saddened he couldn't
see that walking on the moon was something that would
benefit all mankind. "Still, he's very brave. What he's doing
will make a lot of people angry." She touched a finger to the
picture of Reverend Abernathy leading a mule over the
causeway to the Cape, as if that alone would protect him.
The year before, we'd gone back to D.C. for a visit only to
find out when our plane landed that Martin Luther King
had been assassinated. There had been tanks on the Beltway,
smoke in the very neighborhood where Carol and I used to
go to play with our housekeeper's granddaughter.

I put the clipping about the march back in the envelope.
My father had also enclosed a short note on paper headed
A MEMO FROM THE OFFICE OF THE VICE PRESIDENT, which
is what his job was now at the junior college. It had turned
out you couldn't be a real president of a junior college in

Florida, as opposed to an acting one, unless you had a Ph.D. So they hired an outsider to replace Dr. Henry. Now my father had a new boss.

> Your mother took Bertha and Lucky to the vet for their shots. I got gas in both cars today. They say all the visitors will suck the county dry by launch time. The traffic is supposed to be terrible.

This time he'd remembered to sign it *Your father.* Sometimes he forgot and signed his full name as if this were any interoffice memo.

"Did you hear the shot?" I asked Carol.

She nodded. "Coming across the lake. I hear we are all going to get to watch the moon walk on Sunday on TV in the mess hall." Today was Wednesday. It would take Armstrong, Aldrin, and Collins that long to get to the moon.

"Whose TV?" I asked. As far as I knew, the camp didn't have one, though there was talk of a black-and-white portable in the counselors' recreation cabin, a place where there were also rumored to be hot showers and a Coke machine.

Carol shrugged. "Beats me."

While I was talking to Carol, Andy and Celia had gone back to Lakefront, the collection of tents that housed Aquatics, to change. I bought my Clorets and headed after them, cutting through General Registration. It was empty, the campers still at the ball game except for Leemona and Charlotte, who were presumably still at the lake, if not in it. The tents in all the units in the camp were alike, really halfway to being cabins. They all had wooden floors raised off the ground by a good three feet to help keep out armadillos and snakes and other unwelcome creatures. Inside each tent were four iron cots, and over each cot, a mosquito net hanging from a thin wood-and-wire frame. In front of each bed stood the camper's footlocker, which held all the clothes and other personal items the mothers had been told by the camp to pack.

When it wasn't pouring rain, the heavy canvas front, back, and sides of the tents were supposed to be rolled up and tied in a special Girl Scout way. That was the first thing they taught each camper when she arrived. Fresh air discouraged the bugs and the mildew, we were all told, though since the fresh air they were talking about was about ninety-eight degrees with 100 percent humidity, I doubt this helped much. Still everyone did as they were told, so that the tents in a unit usually looked like no more than a collection of cots, trunks, floors, and canvas roofs.

But in General Registration, I couldn't help noticing one tent had all its flaps down and tightly tied, as if we were expecting a hurricane. I stopped and stared, wondering if someone inside was sick, though if that were true, she'd be in the infirmary, another building left over from WPA days. Last summer I had spent a wretched two days there with ten other girls who also had the stomach flu. Then suddenly I knew without being told that the tent was Leemona and Charlotte's. The tent stood out the same way they did. I stopped there, wondering what it was like to feel so out of place in this place. This took some imagination, since I felt so at home here. I imagined Charlotte and Leemona inside on a dark, hot night listening to the armadillos, who were harmless but sounded like rhinos coming through the palmettos. I imagined the other campers in General Registration laughing and pointing as Charlotte and Leemona walked by on their way to the showers. Nothing good is going to come of this, I thought.

SATURDAY AFTER WATER ballet practice, I was the last back at the tent. I'd had to put the record player away, hauling it back to the storage room we called the Glory Hole. Celia and Andy were already dressed in their green shorts and white shirts by the time I got back from the shower. Andy was combing her hair, but Celia was just standing there, her arms crossed and her foot tapping the way it did when she was angry.

She was trying to get Andy to agree to her plan for that

evening's flag ceremony. Our tent was in charge. Celia, of course, was in favor of an elaborate ceremony with much saluting and turning flank left or flank right. I played deaf, gathering up my clothes. I only hoped it wasn't so complicated one of us would drop the flag. My mother had taught me all about flag etiquette and how dropped flags had to be either burned or buried. Buried probably, now that Vietnam War protestors regularly burned flags.

Just then there was a knock on the tent pole. Only counselors knocked, other campers just walked in. It was Happy. "Something's up, Doc," she said. She was a great one for using campers' nicknames. After all, she had to use hers, didn't she? "The camp director wants to see you."

"Me?" I said.

"That's what she said."

"Why?" I couldn't imagine what Mrs. Pratt could want with me. Except for making announcements at dinner, she spent most of her time in the trailer that was her office working on things like payroll and budget, stuff nobody else had to worry about.

"Ours is not to reason why, just to do or die," Happy said.

"Can't I get dressed first?" I was still in my underwear, water dripping from my hair.

"Double-time," Happy said. "Otherwise, you'll miss lunch."

"Yummm," Celia said after Happy left. "Saturday is Spam salad on white bread and potato sticks. Not to mention the usual thawed, leftover Girl Scout cookies." The council had introduced a couple of new kinds of cookies that year, Tahitian Treats and Butter Crinkles, but they had failed to sell like the traditional Thin Mints and Peanut Butter Sandwich cookies. We had them for dessert every day, either at lunch or dinner. Chappy, our cook, had even taken to crumbling them in vanilla pudding and baking them on top of cobblers. Celia rubbed her stomach in mock joy. "I sure wouldn't want to miss that lunch."

I dressed as quickly as I could and went to Mrs. Pratt's office. As I knocked on the door of the trailer, I could see Celia and Andy counting off paces by the flagpole.

"Come on in. It's open," Mrs. Pratt called out, so I did. The trailer had the only air conditioner in the camp, and the air pouring out of the window unit was so cold it hurt. The hair stood up on my arms. After all those days in the sun and nights under my mosquito netting, the idea of wanting cold air constantly blowing on you struck me as unnatural, maybe even unhealthy, an odd thought for a girl raised with central air. I halfway expected to see my breath. Mrs. Pratt looked up from her paperwork and blinked. "Oh," she said, surprised to see a camper and not a counselor. She was not much taller than me and had gray hair that she wore very short, without any permanent wave or hair coloring. Her face was tanned the color and texture of a wrinkled grocery bag. Rumor had it that before she was a professional scout, she'd been a nun.

I tried to imagine Mrs. Pratt in a black-and-white habit like the Flying Nun on TV, but couldn't quite do it. She was wearing a camp T-shirt and shorts and seemed not to notice the cold. Mrs. Pratt was the one who assigned the counselors their nicknames. Campers weren't allowed to know the counselors' real names, though presumably Mrs. Pratt used hers. She waved me to a chair beside her desk. "Cookie?" she said, offering me a Tahitian Treat.

"No, thank you," I said.

Mrs. Pratt took off the half-glasses she'd been using to read and let them dangle by a cord around her neck. "Do you know why I've asked you here?"

"No, ma'am." I had no idea.

"I have a problem and only you can help me. You'd like to help me, wouldn't you?"

I nodded, not wanting to seem rude, but not wanting to commit to a favor without knowing what it was. When Carol and I were little, sprawled out watching TV in the evening, my mother used to ask, "Do you love me?" If either of us said yes, she would invariably add, "Well, then how about getting me my slippers?" This had made me suspicious of seemingly innocent questions.

Mrs. Pratt sighed. "The problem is with our two scholarship students, Leemona Bishop and Charlotte Mintey. You know who they are, don't you?"

I hadn't heard Leemona and Charlotte's last names before, but I nodded again. "Everybody knows," I said.

Mrs. Pratt rubbed her nose where her glasses had rested. "Indeed. Well, the problem is no one in General Registration will be their tentmates. The girls who were assigned there asked to be moved yesterday. There was some disagreement about leaving the tent flaps down at night, I believe, and no one will agree to take their place."

"Hmmm," I said, trying to sound as if I was as worried as she was. Did she want me to suggest a punishment for the General Registration campers who were showing so little unit spirit?

"Of course," she went on, "it's bigger than just tent flaps. There are some girls, I am sad to say, who do not want to sleep in the same tent as a Negro camper."

Especially, I thought, one as unfriendly as Leemona. "Mmmm," I said, shaking my head. I didn't know what advice I could offer. I wasn't a counselor, or even an adult.

Mrs. Pratt put her hand on my arm—her fingers were frigid—and said, "Jesse, I know *you're* not prejudiced." I wondered how she could be so sure. For a second, I thought she had somehow seen the clipping about the poor people's march my father had sent. "Because you've been such a good friend to Celia." I suddenly saw myself the way she saw me—as a camper who obviously had no qualms about accepting a black tentmate. "So, I'm asking you, for the good of the camp, if you would consider moving into Leemona and Charlotte's tent."

I should have seen her request coming a long way off, but I hadn't. I stared at her. Did she understand her own camp enough to know what she was asking me to do? "But Leemona and Charlotte," I said, speaking slowly to be sure of making myself understood, "are in *General Registration*." General Registration where the campers spent their days braiding lanyards and wrapping God's Eyes and learning to sing "Frère Jacques" in rounds.

"Yes," Mrs. Pratt said, "they are."

"And I am in *Aquatics*."

"Well," Mrs. Pratt said, "I think you can still do some activities with your old unit. The water ballet, for instance. I understand from Happy that that is going very well." She squeezed my arm a little. "I know it will be a sacrifice. But do you want Leemona and Charlotte to go home and tell their parents that all the campers at Turtle Lake were prejudiced against them?"

I shook my head. I didn't want Charlotte, especially, to go home thinking that at all. Leemona, it seemed to me, already had her mind made up, but then I would probably have felt about the same if I had been in her place. I didn't know what to say. I wanted Mrs. Pratt to think she had been right about me. I wanted Carol to think I was a good scout, a good person. But did I want to do the right thing enough to go sleep in Charlotte and Leemona's stuffy tent with the babies in General Registration? To give up Celia and Andy as tentmates? To give up Aquatics for arts and crafts and lose my friends in the process?

Mrs. Pratt stood up. "Will you think about it?" she asked. "You can tell me tomorrow after breakfast."

I stood, too. "Okay," I said.

She put her arms out and gave me a stiff little director-like hug.

Stepping into the bright sunlight and heat outside the trailer felt like sleepwalking into a wall. I could barely see. I staggered down the steps. "Left flank, not right!" I heard. "How am I supposed to hand off the flag if your back is toward me?"

"Save me, Doc," Andy called out when she saw me. "She's snapped at last. No one can do this many about-faces without getting motion sickness."

Celia snorted. "Complain, complain, complain. Are we going to run through this one more time before lunch or not?"

"Not," Andy said, shaking her head. She looked at me. "What did Frau Commandant want?"

I told them about Mrs. Pratt needing someone to move in with Leemona and Charlotte.

"How dare she?" Celia said. She looked close to tears.

"She's the director," I said. "She has to think about what's best for the camp." Just then, General Registration trooped by on their way to their Spam salad sandwiches. Leemona and Charlotte brought up the rear like unhappy puppies.

When Celia saw them, she threw the towel she and Andy had been using to practice the flag ceremony on the ground. "They're ruining everything," she said and ran off toward our unit.

Andy watched her go, then turned back to me. "So, what are you going to do?"

"I don't know. I don't want to leave you guys, but . . ." Chappy stepped out the backdoor of the mess hall and rang the bell. Andy just stood there, like there was more to be said. I asked her, "How come Mrs. Pratt didn't ask you to move?"

Andy shrugged, "Maybe she thinks anybody whose dad drives a delivery truck has to be a racist at heart. Maybe she's right. I mean, about not asking me. I wouldn't do it."

"Why not?" I said.

"Because Celia would never forgive me, and she's my friend, not Leemona and Charlotte. Why should I hurt her?"

"Maybe we could all room together," I said. Usually there were only four cots in a tent, two on each side, but sometimes if a unit was crowded they squeezed in an extra one across the back.

"Oh, good," Andy said, "that way when the junior KKK in General Registration wants to burn down a tent with some black campers in it, all of them will be conveniently in the same place."

"No one's going to set the tent on fire."

Andy raised an eyebrow. "Celia might."

Halfway through lunch, Happy and Sneezy stood on their chairs to announce that Sunday was officially declared a Moon Fest in honor of the Apollo 11 mission. For the occasion, they borrowed from the festival we'd had the first session, Hawaii Aloha, and from one we had last year, Chinese New Year. Tomorrow there would be the usual canoe races and bonfire, plus both a luau and Chinese fire drills. After the luau, we would all get to stay up to see the first astronauts, the first Americans, the first men, set foot on the moon, an event that was going to be broadcast live around the world.

Celia skipped lunch, still mad, but Moon Fest was too big an operation for her to ignore. She even canceled water ballet practice for the duration. She was determined Aquatics was going to win the decorated canoe contest with her own special Polynesian design. We would use bamboo poles, she explained, to attach an outrigger to the regulation aluminum canoe. The outrigger would be carved from the same block Styrofoam that kept the swimming dock afloat and then covered with crêpe paper flowers. Celia was so intent on her plans, she let Andy haul down the flag willy-nilly that night without so much as an about-face or salute—a clear sign she had new priorities.

We worked on the canoe all afternoon. I'd hoped for a chance to talk to Carol and ask her whether she thought I should move, but Outpost was cooking out and had not crossed the lake for lunch or dinner. We kept working after dinner, not stopping until after midnight, our hands sore from twisting crêpe paper into red-and-yellow hibiscus. That night I lay on my cot in the dark, too tired to go to sleep.

Usually the three of us would talk. Celia liked to hear me go on and on about something—say the giant heads on Easter Island or why Hawaiians ate poi. Anything I remembered, or thought I did, from all the books I'd read. "My, my," Celia would say, and, "Amazing!" These late-night lectures were why she had nicknamed me Doc. She said I knew as much as any professor. On the other hand, Andy tended to drift off early in these discussions, after snorting a few times like she wasn't altogether convinced of my sources.

When I was really on a talking jag, I could go on half the night, one subject leading to another, until I fell asleep, drained of all thought.

Tonight, my last night in the tent if I was moving tomorrow, we were all quiet. Andy was snoring softly, asleep the minute she got her mosquito netting tucked in. Celia, though, I could tell was awake and so was probably quiet either because she was still mad at me or because her head was full of Moon Fest plans. She had made up a team name, the Dragons, and a chant, which was to be done to the tune of "I'm a Little Teapot." With appropriate accompanying gestures, it went:

I'm a little dragon, green and stout.
Here is my tail, and here is my snout.
When I get all worked up, here me shout:
All the way, Dragons, make the other teams pout!

I wasn't thinking about the Moon Fest. I was thinking about Leemona and Charlotte and whether one white Girl Scout could really do anything to change the world. Once when I was in kindergarten, I'd gone into D.C. with my mother and seen a sign posted in a restaurant window. I asked my mother what it said. "Whites Only," she told me. She had clearly been embarrassed and explained both the sign's purpose and her disapproval of it. I remembered being mostly puzzled. "But if we won't let them come in our restaurants, then they might not let us go in theirs," I said.

My mother shook her head. "You wouldn't want to eat in theirs, honey," she'd said.

By the time I was in first grade in Maryland, I always had one or two black kids in my class. In Cocoa, probably a third of my junior high school was black. Two of our six cheerleaders were black. I got the feeling Miss Jepson was careful to be sure that was always the case. Since elementary school we'd been tracked into Advanced, Regular, and Basic classes. Somehow the only black kids who were routinely in more than my PE class or homeroom were two sisters whose father was a doctor. They were my friends, but out of the hundred or so of the other black kids, I could probably only name four or five. The rest were just faces, dark faces, people I didn't see when I walked the hall looking for people I knew. The black kids I didn't know seemed to look right through me, my blond hair and pale skin, as if I wasn't any more real to them than they were to me. At school there just didn't seem to be any way through that wall, but here, with Leemona and Charlotte, didn't I have a chance to break through?

I turned on my back, then my side, then my stomach, then my back again, trying to puzzle it out. I could hear Celia turning, too. There was an art to sleeping at camp.

You had to lie stiff and straight, hands firmly at your sides. If any part of your body—your knee, a hand—touched the mosquito netting while you were asleep, in the morning you would have a crop of evenly spaced bites where the mosquitos had been feasting on you through the netting all night. So Celia, like me, was not so much tossing about in bed as spinning in place. She was clearly restless. "Doc?" she whispered. "Are you awake?"

She didn't sound angry, but it was hard to be sure. I considered pretending I was asleep, but in the end I answered, "Yeah."

"How can you like those scholarship girls more than me?" she asked, her voice tight. She was still pissed at me.

I opened my mouth to say she had it all wrong, that she was my friend, not them, that I was acting out of a sense of duty, of justice. But then how she'd asked, not even using Leemona and Charlotte's names, made me angry. "How come you *don't* like them?"

"Why should I?" she said. "It's not like they've gone out of their way to be nice to me."

"You haven't exactly been sweetness and light to Charlotte and Leemona either."

"Why should I be? Do I have to automatically like everyone with dark skin and kinky hair?" she said. "Is that what you think? Like because you're both white you should like

Janet Dobbins?" Janet Dobbins was a girl in Campcraft who had pointed at my odd feet one day when we were walking down the hill to lunch and said, "Hey, camper, can you quack too?"

"No," I said, "but Leemona and Charlotte didn't call you a duck."

"Just their being here makes me look bad," she said. "Scholarship kids in their charity bathing suits. People like that"—she was getting worked up now—"people like *Reverend* Ralph Abernathy going on TV leading a mule and a bunch of raggedy nobodies to a space launch where there are senators and men who've won Nobel prizes, not to mention Walter Cronkite, all staring at them. They just tell everybody in the world that black people are no better than trash, no better than poor ignorant trash. That we're all poor. That we all need charity. My daddy is paying for me to go to camp, just like yours is. My mother took me out shopping before I came and bought me two *new* bathing suits. We don't need any charity. We're not poor." She was breathing hard, almost wheezing, she was so angry. I could hear it even over Andy's snoring.

"But Celia," I said, "Leemona and Charlotte can't help it if they're poor."

"Yes, they can. They can go to school and stay there. Then they can have good jobs. My father says so. Then they can send their kids anywhere they want. Nobody in America has to be poor." I had never been poor, but my mother had as a child, I guess, at least compared to my father. She might have gone to camp on a scholarship, if she had ever had the chance. After his father lost all his money, my father had gone to West Point on what amounted to a government-paid free ride.

"So are you still going to do it?" Celia pressed. "Move, I mean?"

Then I knew for sure. Moving was the right thing. "Yes," I said.

"Go to General Registration then," she said. "Go to hell."

"Likewise," I said, turning my back toward her. I could be angry, too.

15

The next morning, I slept in. Partly to avoid Chappie's Sunday breakfast of oatmeal and stewed prunes, mostly to avoid Celia. When Happy stuck her head in the tent to say Mrs. Pratt wanted to see me in her trailer, I was just getting dressed. I hadn't packed my trunk yet, but I figured it wouldn't take me long. Maybe Leemona would help me carry it over to General Registration. If not Leemona, Andy. I felt calm, sure of my decision.

The trailer was still frigid inside. "Please sit," Mrs. Pratt said. I sat, the metal folding chair like ice on the back of my legs. She sighed. "I'm afraid I was premature in talking to you yesterday. I spoke with Leemona and Charlotte, and they don't want another tentmate."

I blinked. "Leemona . . ." I started.

Mrs. Pratt held up her hand. "Actually," she pursed her lips, then unpursed them, as if I was forcing her to say more than she wanted, "it was Charlotte who objected."

I stared at Mrs. Pratt. *Charlotte?*

"I knew about this before she came," Mrs. Pratt said, "but I thought at camp, well . . ." Mrs. Pratt shrugged. "Charlotte's father gave permission for her to come, but Charlotte lives with her grandmother, apparently a very old-fashioned woman. She doesn't allow whites in her house. Leemona said she didn't care one way or the other about your moving in, but Charlotte started crying and said she liked you, but she couldn't sleep if there was a white person in the bed next to her. She said she was sorry, but that was the way she felt."

I sat there stunned, not knowing what to say. I'd wanted to be seen as a hero, now I felt like a fool. "I'm sorry, Jesse," Mrs. Pratt said, standing to see me out.

Outside, the camp was buzzing with preparations for the Moon Fest. Marly walked by carrying a brush and can of paint. Rumor was, Masquerade was our main competition in the decorated canoe contest. Should I pump Marly about their plans, I wondered, and report what I found to Celia? Celia, oh God. What was I going to say to Celia about why I wasn't moving? She was going to ask me. I wished now I hadn't told her about it at all. I didn't want her laughing at me or making fun of Charlotte. The last shouldn't have bothered me—it was Charlotte who didn't want me around —but I felt protective of her. She was as afraid of me as she was of the lake and the armadillos.

"You girls!" It was Chappie. Marly put down her can of paint and went over. I followed. "You're drafted. I need two pairs of quick young hands to help me," Chappie said. She put us to work on the fortune cookies for the luau. Happy had typed out little slips of paper that said things like *Confucius say: A Good Scout Is Loyal and True,* or, the one that struck home with me, *Confucius Say: Make New Friends but Keep the Old.* Chappie showed Marly and me how to put the fortunes between two Tahitian Treats and glue them together with a little dab from a giant silver can of U.S. Department of Agriculture Surplus Peanut Butter. Being with Marly felt like the old days in fifth and sixth grade. I told her what had happened with Charlotte, about Charlotte's grandmother.

"My grandmother can't stand black people," Marly said, meaning her father's mother who lived in Alabama, not her abuela, her mother's mother, who still lived in Cuba. "She certainly wouldn't let one in the house who wasn't her maid or some kind of repairman. When Bill Cosby was on the cover of *TV Guide* for being in *I Spy,* Grammy cut out his face before she'd let the magazine in the house. She said just the thought of black people on TV made her sick." Marly stuck a few more cookies together. "So why does it seem so weird to you that Charlotte's grandma would feel the same way about white people?"

I tried to pin down what I did think. I thought about Martin Luther King suffering in the Birmingham jail like a saint, the students on the freedom rides getting beaten but never raising a hand. "I guess I thought blacks were better than us." Or at least I had thought that of Charlotte.

Marly raised her eyebrows. "What, like they aren't human?"

After that, I wormed out of Marly that Masquerade was building a volcano out of papier mâché in the middle of their canoe and were planning to use a bug bomb to spew real smoke during the water parade.

I didn't see Celia until lunch, when she and Andy came in. I thought she would ignore me, but instead she sat right next to me. "Wait until you hear the news," she said, raising her eyebrows. Before she could say another word, Mrs. Pratt rang the little bell she used to call for silence. She announced that, sadly, two campers, Leemona Bishop and Charlotte Mintey, would be going home later that afternoon. Celia poked me. Somehow she had known. My first reaction—relief—was not noble. If Charlotte and Leemona were leaving, then no one, not even Celia or Andy, would have to know they'd refused to have me as a tentmate.

Mrs. Pratt sat down, leaving the camp to guess why, with only one week to go, Leemona and Charlotte were leaving. But Andy had gotten the full story out of Sneezy. Celia nodded as Andy told the story. That morning after breakfast, Andy said, Sneezy had taken Charlotte to the end of the dock to watch the teams practicing for the canoe races. Sneezy had tied Charlotte into a life vest just in case she fell or got knocked into the water. Instead, Charlotte, looking down as usual, had let the glasses, without which she couldn't see her own hand in front of her face, slip off her nose and disappear into the muddy water of Turtle Lake.

By the time Sneezy realized why Charlotte was crying so inconsolably, the canoes had reached the dock and ten teams of girls were wading where Charlotte's glasses had taken their plunge. In spite of Sneezy's best efforts, no one could find them. Andy and Celia had missed seeing any of this firsthand because they had been too busy madly hairpinning the last paper garlands to the Styrofoam outrigger of our unit's decorated canoe. According to Sneezy, Charlotte had been so upset, the nurse gave her a shot. When Mrs. Pratt called her, Charlotte's grandmother had a reaction that was almost as severe. Mrs. Pratt had offered to personally buy Charlotte a new pair of glasses, but Charlotte's grandmother and then Leemona's parents had demanded the immediate return of their girls.

Celia shrugged as if none of this interested her much. Last-minute adjustments had to be made to the canoe. "Good riddance," she said, with a flip of her hand.

I wanted to slap her. It didn't feel over to me. I wanted to see Charlotte one last time, maybe to prove to her I wasn't like other white campers. Maybe to show her I was a better, more forgiving, person than she was. So after lunch, while the Aquatics canoe, paddled by Andy and Happy, was competing in the floating parade, I went looking for Leemona and Charlotte. Mrs. Pratt was loading their trunks into the camp's station wagon. I could hear the Dragon cheer being chanted full tilt as our glorious if slightly top-heavy outrigger canoe made its ceremonial circle of the lake. I watched as Mrs. Pratt slammed the back of the station wagon shut then wiped her hands on her shorts. She saw me standing there, one foot digging at the sandy ground.

"It's probably all for the best," she said, patting me on the back, as if something terribly unfortunate had happened to me, too, and not just to Charlotte. Then the nurse came out of the infirmary leading blind and weeping Charlotte by the arm. Behind them came the assistant director, Chipmunk, with one hand firmly on Leemona's shoulder, as if she were under arrest.

"Watch that last step," I heard the nurse say to Charlotte just as she tripped down it.

As Charlotte passed, I leaned forward and started to say, "Charlotte, I'm sorry," but she jumped, as if the white blur of my face was what she saw in her nightmares. She began crying even harder. The nurse hurried her past me toward the waiting car. At just that moment, Celia came walking up. Seeing her, Leemona shrugged free of Chipmunk's grasp and stepped forward. She pushed her face into Celia's, her fists clenched at her sides.

"Bitch," Leemona said.

Celia stood with her hands in her pockets, looking relaxed, like Leemona's nose wasn't a half-inch from hers, like none of this mattered. "Bitchette," she said, in a tone that made it a joke.

Leemona stepped back. The nurse was trying to help Charlotte into the station wagon, but Charlotte had stopped dead in her tracks. "Leemona?" she called, looking blankly left and right.

Then Leemona laughed, as if she got the joke at last. "Bitchette," she repeated, as if trying out a new word. Leemona crooked a finger, beckoning Celia to listen, as if she had some secret Celia alone could share. Curious in spite of herself, Celia leaned toward her. Leemona whispered, "Don't kid yourself, honey, you're a nigger, too." Then Leemona helped Charlotte into the station wagon, and Chipmunk drove off in a cloud of white, choking sand. For a moment,

Celia just stood there, her expression unchanged. Suddenly, I was afraid for her. I'd been mad at her for all the things she refused to see, now I wanted to hide them again. I felt ashamed.

"Celia?" I said.

Celia turned her head to one side and shook it, like she was clearing lake water from one ear. Then, as if Leemona had left without saying a word, Celia turned on one heel and said, "Let's go see if our canoe won."

We had won: Blue ribbon, Best Decorated Canoe. Marly's unit, Masquerade, came in second. Apparently, the volcano hadn't been firmly lashed to their canoe. They might have won if it hadn't fallen into the water near the end of the parade. When Celia and I got there, the rest of the girls in Aquatics were cheering madly. They had Andy and Happy up on their shoulders and had started a stumbling, triumphal march toward our tents, Andy's long legs trailing the ground.

Outpost had been too cool to enter the decorated canoe contest, but they won the canoe races and so were in charge of that night's bonfire. Rather, my sister Carol was. Though she was allergic to wood smoke along with most everything else, she loved a good fire. She had built up a log cabin fire out of huge pieces of pine. The thing looked almost big enough for Abe Lincoln to have been born in it. At her signal, a flaming wad of kerosene-soaked sanitary napkin shot down a wire from the top of the flagpole, and the log cabin burst into flames. Carol had outdone herself. "Oooh," we all said, and "aaah," as awed by this feat as the outside world, glued to their televisions, had been by the Lunar Module's touchdown on the Sea of Tranquility earlier in the afternoon. While the world waited and waited for word that Armstrong and Aldrin were ready to leave the LM, we campers held hands and sang the usual mix of Beatles hits and Girl Scout camp songs.

We all poured into the mess hall at about ten-thirty that night, ready first for luau and then the moon walk. Chappie had repeated her Hawaii Aloha feast. There was deviled Spam molded into the shape of roast suckling pigs with candied crab apples in their mouths. Stacks of white bread took the place of poi, and there were big platters of canned pineapple. For dessert, of course, we had the fortune cookies.

Celia tossed a pineapple ring at me. Everyone settled down and was digging into the Spam, making sandwiches. Usually we ate dinner at six, and so after a whole day of Moon Fest, we were really starving. "It's starting!" someone up front called, and I looked up to see Mrs. Pratt adjusting the rabbit ears on a very small black-and-white TV, undoubtedly the secret set from the counselors' rec cabin. First there was snow. Then a shot of something alternately very

black and very white, which Walter Cronkite's voice said
was the surface of the moon and one of the legs of the Lunar
Module. Armstrong would descend the ladder first, Cronkite
said—his voice as familiar after all these years as my own
father's—"in just a few more historic minutes."

I moved closer to the TV, abandoning my sandwich. I'd
been waiting for this moment all my life. I sat on the concrete floor staring up at the small screen. There was a sudden crackle of static, then Armstrong backed out of the LM.
Behind me the room went wild, girls cheering and tossing
cookies at each other, even though all Armstrong had done
so far was awkwardly climb a few rungs down the ladder,
looking a lot like one of those miniature helmeted divers
people kept in their aquariums. He was saying something,
making some kind of speech, but the noise behind me
drowned it out. Then he was down, walking around on the
moon like a kid in snow boots. We had done it.

President Kennedy and Marly's dad and everybody who
worked at the Cape and in Houston, and every family who
paid taxes—together we had done it. Nothing from now
on would be the same. They would probably start the calen-
dar over. This would be the last day of 1969 P.M. (Pre-
Moonwalk). Tomorrow would be the first day of the year
1 A.M. (After Moonwalk). What will it be like for the babies
being born around the world tonight? They would probably

grow up taking vacations on the moon. They'd have a hard time realizing what all the fuss had been about.

"It doesn't look real." Andy slid onto the floor next to me. She was watching Aldrin, out of the lander now, kicking up moon dust. "I mean, how do we know this isn't just happening out in the desert in Arizona or somewhere?"

I stared at her. No wonder her father drove a chip truck. No wonder the psychic grandmothers of Casa Dega bought snack food from him and cookies from his daughter. She was tuned to the wrong channel.

Happy switched on a record player, and Celia started leading a conga line. No one was watching the TV anymore but me and Andy, and Andy was making those snorting noises like she did when she listened, disbelieving, to me talk late into the night.

It was all too much. I stood up. "I gotta pee," I said, but I headed not to the bathroom but out into the night. I wanted to see the moon. To see if somehow, in some way I couldn't quite define, it looked different. Earlier, a big silver slice of the moon had been hanging low in the sky. Now, there was no moon at all. It must have set. Someday soon, I was sure, whole cities would be on the moon, jeweled necklaces lighting up the dry, dusty craters and seas. Now the moon was hiding, ashamed somehow of the two men making tracks on its surface. Men and footprints too tiny to be seen from where I stood, even if the moon had been full and bright.

I wondered what Leemona was thinking, and Charlotte. Were they at home watching the moon walk on their own TVs? Did it seem possible to them that their children might someday live on the moon? Or did they look up at night and see only white?

"Jes—" It was Carol. She had been down at the site of the bonfire, making sure the ashes were all safely buried. "Is that you?"

"It's me, all right." I said. I must have sounded as blue as I felt because she stopped next to me. She smelled strongly of smoke.

"Are you okay?" she asked.

"Yeah," I said. She put her arm around my shoulder. "Thanks," I said. She nodded.

We stood there for a long time, two sisters looking up at a black sky.

16 October 1970

One Saturday, Carol and her best friend, Stephanie, marched into the mall bookstore and bought a paperback copy of *Everything You Always Wanted to Know About Sex but Were Afraid to Ask*. They let everyone they knew sign up for a turn with the book. Everybody but me.

All I knew was that suddenly everyone was laughing at things I didn't find funny, telling jokes I didn't get. Then on Friday, Carol came up to me in the lunchroom during fourth period begging for my help. Carol had been supposed to pass the book to Pete Orsini but had left it in her desk in Madame Muller's classroom. Madame Muller was our French teacher, a woman who steadfastly refused to admit that there were French names for parts of the body. Stephanie, Carol said, would kill her when she found out she'd lost the book, not to mention Pete. Since I had French III next period, it was up to me, her only sister, to save her.

"You can do it," she said.

I stood with my arms crossed. "Why should I?" I said, upset she'd left me out of the only illicit thing she'd ever done in her life.

Carol sighed. "I'll let you read the book."

I nodded. "Deal."

"It's under the third seat from the door," she said, leaving me with a firm squeeze of my shoulder.

It wasn't easy to get away with sitting at a different desk in a class that had only four bored inmates. But I did it, making a show of finding gum stuck to my usual seat and moving to the one where Carol said she'd sat. Then I waited until the lights were off and Madame Muller was showing French Impressionist slides.

In the dim light, I slumped down in the desk, groping among the old gum and papers for the book. "Camille Pisarro's *Place du Théâtre Français,* painted in 1898," Madame Muller read from the booklet that came with the slides. "Notice the panorama of blurred dark figures against a light background." The slide projector clicked. A fuzzy scene of a street full of people and wagons appeared. My fingers found the book, closed around it. I slipped it out of the desk and into my lap. Madame Muller went on, reading the description of the next painting before she changed slides, "Édouard Manet's *Le Déjeuner sur l'Herbe,* painted in 1863. Notice the combination of a modern setting with traditional sixteenth-century Italian themes." Carol and Stephanie had ripped off the real jacket and recovered the book with yellow-and-orange flowered contact paper, and Magic Markered *Betty Crocker's Hot Dishes* on the spine, another joke I didn't get. "Contemporary viewers," Madame Muller said, "found the portrayal of a nude woman and two clothed men shocking." *Click,* FLASH. The screen was blank, and the flood of light made me sit up, afraid of getting caught.

Madame went on. "Edgar Degas's *Ballet Rehearsal (Adagio),* painted in 1874. Notice his use of arrested motion," she said, and *click,* some leaping ballerinas appeared, very like ones I remembered from my third-grade tour of the National Gallery of Art. I pretended to be interested in the blurry, bluish montage of tutus and toe shoes. "Edgar Degas's *The Morning Bath,*" she announced, and *click,* there was another bright, empty blank. Stephen, the only boy in the class, raised his hand. Stephen was president of the French Club (a true losers' organization) and the only student with any enthusiasm left for French after three years of Madame Muller. The rest of us sincerely wished we had taken Spanish.

"Pardon, Madame," Stephen said, rolling his *r.* "There isn't any picture on the screen."

"Of course not, Stephen," murmured Madame Muller, pronouncing his name with a soft *ph* in the middle, which suited Stephen, so soft and plump, too well. "I would *never* show *nudes* in mixed company."

So she went on, showing or not showing us the Impressionist masters. When a blank screen gave me enough light to read, I flipped open the book. *Breasts are erotic . . .*

Then a landscape came on, and I lost my place in the gloom. *Click,* FLASH. More light. *The size of the penis does not . . .*

Three dim landscapes in a row, and I fumbled. We were moving on, she announced, to the Postimpressionists. "Paul Cézanne's *La Montagne Sainte-Victoire,*" Madame Muller droned, "notice the . . ." *Click,* FLASH. We got back to more censored nakedness. By the light of Madame Muller's invisible nudes, I caught my first knee-weakening glimpses of the words *penis, vagina,* and *orgasm.* My tiny nipples sat up in the padded bomb shelters of my bra and begged.

I went straight home from the bus and locked myself in the bathroom. I sat down on the toilet and opened the book to the title page. Yes, I had been afraid to ask. It was true. I remembered hearing two ninth graders whispering in the second-floor girls' lavatory:

"So she lay down in the middle of the bed," the first one had breathed out, mascara-clumped eyes wide.

"Unh-huh, unh-huh," the second murmured through Pony Pink lips.

"And she says to the guy, 'Do you know what I want?'"

"Unh-huh." The second girl chewed on her rattail comb.

"And he says, 'No.' So she spreads her legs even wider and says, 'Now do you know what I want?' and . . ."

"Unh-huh."

"So he says, 'Yeah, you want the whole damn bed.'" The black rattail comb clattered to the floor as the two girls collapsed, clinging convulsively to the sinks, but I hadn't gotten it. Not really.

I speed-read the first chapter of the book. A man has a penis. Okay. I'd seen Paul's in the flesh, and my second favorite book up to this point hadn't been *Fifty Centuries of Art* for nothing. I'd seen my share of naked marble men. A woman, the book said, had a vagina. I knew that, too, though more vaguely. I had it confused with a womb and maybe also with my bladder. Were there really separate envelopes inside me for sex, babies, and pee? It seemed so. A woman was also supposed to have a clitoris. *Cly-toris, cleet-oris, clito-rees*? It was as bad as the names in *The Lord of the Rings,* my first favorite book. I sincerely wished Dr. Reuben had followed J.R.R. Tolkien's lead and included a few good maps with the points of interest done in red.

Exploration was called for, so I got into the bath. I'd

spent fourteen years soaping up what my mother called my fixtures, and I felt sure I knew the territory pretty well, but . . . there it was. However you pronounced it, I did indeed have a clitoris. Round, shy, it peaked and wavered like the soft foot of a winkle at low tide. *Hello, in there, hello.*

AFTER READING *Everything You Always Wanted to Know About Sex,* I understood why I blushed and my nipples stood up around boys that I liked and why I had dreamed about floating in space with Paul. I had lived fourteen years without a clue. I was sure I was the last human being on the planet to find out about sex. I may have been smart, but I was retarded. Dr. Reuben, who wrote about six-year-old girls masturbating with their teddy bears, certainly would have thought so.

Now I saw the world with new eyes. I saw vibrators for sale in the drugstore and knew that in spite of the picture on the box, they weren't entirely for massaging feet. When the kids at school told dirty jokes, I got the punch lines. More than that, I saw clearly that everything was a potential dirty joke. Even things that didn't breathe were all about sex. Anything longer than it was tall (bananas, tampons, the Washington Monument) were really just penises. Carol saw it, too. "Will you look at the size of that rocket?" she said one day, holding up *Time* with a Saturn V on the cover. *Penis,* I knew she was thinking. *Really BIG penis.*

"No wonder astronauts are men," I said. Carol laughed so hard she choked.

It was more than that. It was as if the whole world had only been pretending certain things were important—science, art, politics, religion—when actually everyone was only interested in one thing, something not on that list. *Sex.* All the books I'd been reading without really understanding (*War and Peace, The Sun Also Rises,* the James Bond novels I'd snuck from my dad) were really all about sex. Everyone was having sex. Everyone except me.

17 December 1972

Carol and I are on the roof waiting for the moon rocket to blast off. This is not a dream or a science fiction story. We are staying up to see Apollo 17, the last lunar mission, and the only one to leave earth at night. It is pitch-black.

It is supposed to go up at ten, then around eleven, but the countdown keeps getting stopped, the launch time delayed. At first, mothers as well as kids are on top of the other houses in our neighborhood. Most of the fathers are at the Cape, trying to get the rocket up. By the third time the radio announces the countdown has stopped, the mothers are gone, sure the mission is scrubbed.

Up on the roof, the countdown resumes. I think about our mother asleep right under my butt. Although it's past midnight, my father is still at the office, working late as usual on some interminable report. I close my eyes and imagine my parents' dark cherry-wood bed, my mother completely, un-naturally still. When we were little, she used to yell in her sleep, No no no! By this night, she is not only on Valium, she is mixing it with bourbon, and so doesn't do that or much else anymore.

At twelve-thirty, Carol says she is giving up. This is not a slumber party, but still she hates staying up late. I beg her to stay, afraid I will have to go, too. I'm sixteen, not a little kid anymore, but still she thinks she is my mother. At least, she thinks somebody should be.

She opens her mouth to say something: *Yes, I will stay. No, I won't.* But I realize I can see her mouth, and I wonder where the light is coming from, and in the same instant I know. The rocket is blasting off, rising over the river like the sun, that bright. I look at the orange trees and see colors, green leaves, waxy white blossoms, yellow fruit sooty with mildew. Above the flame, the sky turns a perfect, ordinary blue. Birds begin to sing. Somewhere, a dog barks.

Then the sound hits us, a roar so loud it makes my bones itch, louder than any rock concert I have yet been allowed to go to. Carol and I are on our feet, hugging each other on the gently sloped roof. She is shouting, and I am shouting, though we can't hear our own voices. The red-and-gold trail burns through the sky, and we track it with our eyes. Our bodies lean forward, longing to follow. But we can't. We are not old enough or strong enough or desperate enough to break free. Gravity will not let us go. Not yet.

In the fading light as the rocket passes downrange, we see who is on the next roof: David Mize and the Hecht boys, one my age, one older than Carol. Over them is a cloud of smoke. They are smiling and waving a bottle at us. They are obviously stoned. All over Brevard County people are either stoned or selling or sorting or smuggling pot. Our senior class president has just been arrested for dealing, though he had to go to Orlando to get busted. No one ever seems to get arrested in Cocoa. At that moment, Brevard County is the drug-smuggling capital of Florida, maybe the drug capital of the United States. But I have never smoked pot or even a cigarette. Partly that is Carol's doing. Or maybe it is all her doing.

"Oh, it's just Jesse Lee," I hear one of them say my name, mocking me for not being with them. I have already gone through my first two years of high school without being allowed in the rest room, Dealer Central. But they don't mock Carol. She does not drink, smoke, take drugs, or chew gum, and they respect the fierceness of her convictions. All those things are bad for your voice, and she is serious about her voice. Carol starts to lift her hand, wave back. Then, as the roar fades, she doesn't. The light dies.

We get down off the roof and back into the air-conditioned

silence of the house, where our mother is sleeping. Carol is shaking her head, her long, arched nose a study in determination. I think her nose is beautiful. I think she is beautiful and strong. She is the one who demands that we act like a family, put up a Christmas tree, eat in the dining room on Thanksgiving, when my father would rather stay at his office, I in my room, my mother in her bed. At that moment, I love her more than anything in the world.

"Remember," she says, "in our family, we don't do things like that."

18

The Friday night after the Apollo 17 launch was the Cocoa High School production of *Oklahoma!* Carol was singing lead alto. This was not a named part. She had been going to try out for the female lead, but Mr. Bright, her chorus teacher, whom she loved with all the fierce loyalty of which she was capable, had told her he needed her in the chorus. Where would he be, he said, without his lead alto? Probably he said this looking into her eyes, maybe with one hand on her shoulder, thumb resting at the base of her neck. He touched when he talked and kissed people hello and good-bye. I imagined Carol nodding, agreeing with whatever he said.

Because of rehearsals, Carol had been gone every night for the last two weeks. She'd wandered around the house singing the alto parts to "Surrey with the Fringe on Top" until the soprano parts, which carry the melody, sounded weird to me. She'd bought the fabric for a pink gingham dress and white petticoat and paid Mrs. Boggs to sew it up for her. (Our mom hadn't used her sewing machine in years.) Mr. Bright had also declared everyone had to wear cowboy boots, lest the production lack authenticity. Carol had very narrow feet (7AAAA) and so had to borrow my father's Bank Americard to special-order a pair. They arrived by mail, finally. Too late for the dress rehearsal, too late for me to see them, but just in time for this, the opening night.

My father came home at five for the first time in months. Since he wore a suit and tie to the office, he was ready to go. My mother, though, was having a tougher time. She managed to get up and get dressed in a blue-and-white pants suit that was only a little too small, but when I came into her room she was sitting on the edge of the bed in her stocking feet.

"I can't seem to find any shoes," she said. Her hair was flat on one side from her pillow, and her green eyes looked as foggy and startled as our cat Lucky's did if somebody shoved him off the dining-room table, his favorite napping place. Lucky was nearly twelve now, with cataracts so bad he could hardly see. When he stumbled blindly out into the backyard, the mockingbirds mobbed him, pulling out hair for their nests, leaving him with bald patches. My mother didn't look much better. I wanted to pet her, to smooth her gray hair the way I would Lucky's or at least give her a hug, but I was also embarrassed by how helpless she looked. Instead I got down on my hands and knees and hunted under the bed for something for her to wear besides slippers.

Ordinarily Carol would have been the one getting her dressed, but Carol was already at the theater, getting made up. "Did you try the closet?" my mother asked, naming the one place where, in my own messy room, I never put my shoes.

"Not yet," I said, standing up, brushing the dust off the knees of my panty hose, "but I will." On the top shelf, I found two pairs of orthopedic pumps, one white and one bone, still in their boxes. My mother had gotten them from the same company specializing in long, narrow feet that had sent Carol her boots. "Here," I said, choosing the white ones, "just the ticket." I knew she didn't want to go out in the world where people could look at her, but this was for Carol. My mother slipped her feet into her new shoes.

Oklahoma! was being staged in the multitorium of my father's junior college. It was a multitorium, my father had explained, because the Baptists in the legislature up in Tallahassee had forbidden the use of state money to build theaters. It had red plush theater seats, an orchestra pit, and orange-pink-and-green carpet my father had chosen because he figured it would never show stains or wear.

An usherette, a girl from the junior chorus, showed my

father, my mother, me, and Carol's boyfriend, Peter, to our seats. I saw the Boggses sitting two rows down and Mrs. Maltezo and Lynn in the first row. Nearly everyone I knew was there. It was the first time Peter had done anything with our family. Carol had arranged this, making my father buy the extra ticket. It felt very significant, also odd. I sat there hoping people who didn't know better would think Peter was my date. He had light brown hair and was thought cute, although what Carol seemed to like best about him was that he was diabetic and had to inject himself with insulin twice a day. She found this both tragic and appealing.

The school band began the overture. The audience applauded as the curtain went up to reveal hay bales and a front porch that was not attached to any house. Tonti Treppler, our future homecoming queen, sang tenderly of the absent Bill Larson, our class treasurer. Bill danced up behind her in cowboy boots. Tonti turned, swinging her skirt. They were playing at being in love. Since elementary school, Tonti and Bill had heartily disliked each other, a fact that everyone but Mr. Bright knew, so it was not good casting. I yawned, waiting for Carol. Peter stirred restlessly beside me. Mother was asleep, slumped discreetly in her seat. I hoped Peter didn't notice. Where was Carol?

Finally, the chorus started singing low and offstage. I heard Carol's voice. I could always hear her voice. I told her this once, after her first chorus concert back in junior high, thinking it was a compliment. She was furious. "You did not," she said. "The mark of a good alto is that it *blends*." Still, I heard her, each note clear and strong as the chorus came trooping across the back of the stage behind the hay bales. Then I saw her, and my heart stopped.

Someone, in a hurry to make up the whole cast, had sprayed her long blond hair a sticky gray to kill the shine and had drawn a single dark eyebrow across her forehead above her long nose. The pink calico dress looked fine, was just Carol's color, or would have been if her hair were its usual blond. The real problem was her boots. Big, mud brown, they looked more like waders than cowboy boots. The chorus hoedowned across the stage, arms swinging, deep in song, but above it everyone could hear Carol's boots. *Clump, thud, clump, thud.* Peter froze in his seat beside me. I felt my face turning red. *Clump.*

Carol had made a terrible mistake. I watched, sweating with a sympathy so strong it was as if we were twins or even the same person. Then I remembered stepping off the bus holding hands with Marly Boggs our first day of junior high. Kids had stared, a couple of boys had laughed, and now I felt a flash of anger toward Carol. She was my older sister. She had certain responsibilities. She should have warned me about holding hands with girls once you were out of sixth grade. And she shouldn't be wearing those ugly, loud boots. She had been my only protection, and I could feel her social standing dropping like a thermometer in an ice bath. All over the multitorium, people were laughing.

Thud. In line behind Carol was Lulu Felton, a fat, legally blind girl in thick tinted glasses who was obviously moving her mouth without singing, clear proof of the lax standards for membership in this chorus. Lulu and Carol passed with lowered eyes behind the beautiful Tonti. *Clump.* I couldn't believe it. Carol had trusted Mr. Bright, her adored teacher, and he had done this to her. Lulu stepped on Carol's heels. The chorus crossed into the wings and disappeared. The boots echoed back, *thud.*

After the performance, my parents and I went backstage, Peter in tow, to see Carol. Peter looked embarrassed to be seen with us. Carol had changed from her calico dress into her blue jeans but was still wearing her makeup, which looked even worse under the fluorescent lights in the gang dressing room. She ran up to us barefoot, her boots in one hand. She took Peter's arm firmly in hers.

"So what did you think?" she asked. Peter smiled faintly at her, then shrugged.

My father, who hated musicals, said, "It was very professionally staged."

"You know you have a beautiful voice, Carol," my

mother, who had once had a beautiful voice herself, said. "You don't need us to tell you that."

Carol nodded, then looked at me. I didn't want to say anything about her performance at all. "Here," I said, taking her boots from her. "If you're staying for the cast party, I'll take these home for you." I was afraid she might put them back on. I thought I could manage to leave them where they would never be found again, like maybe the ditch on the edge of the parking lot.

Carol's cheeks flushed as though she could read my mind. She rubbed the bridge of her nose, smearing her black mono-brow across her forehead. She said, "Fine. Put them in my closet."

A SOUND AT my window woke me. Someone was knocking on one of the jalousies as if it were the door. "Jesse!" I cranked open the window, almost catching whoever was there in the head. It was Peter. He was standing with a flashlight in one hand. When he and Carol had left for the opening night party, he still looked faintly embarrassed. Now it was late, and he just looked worried.

"Um, hi," he said. "Your sister isn't feeling very well." I stood there for a moment, warm air pouring in through the window. I considered that I might be dreaming. Then I heard the central air cut on.

"Give me a minute," I said. I threw on some clothes and went outside. It was another moonless night.

He told me Carol was down on our dock. He turned on his flashlight, and I followed him. Actually it wasn't our dock. It belonged to the neighborhood civic association, to all the people who lived in Luna Heights and kept up with their annual dues. One summer, the fathers (but not my father) had gotten together and built the dock out of pilings stolen by Mr. Heck, who worked for the phone company. A long flight of stairs led down a steep, overgrown bank to the stinking water.

I found Carol hanging off the end of the dock throwing up. Peter's flashlight flickered over an amazing array of empty bottles. I caught sight of a couple of labels. STRAW-BERRY RIPPLE. SMIRNOFF VODKA. He kicked one of the bottles into the water. "It was quite a party." He sounded proud of Carol.

"Yeah," Carol said, her voice echoing from under the dock. It sounded remarkably cheerful. Then she gagged and was sick again. I knelt and took one of Carol's ankles. Peter took the other. We sat looking down into the water. After a while, Peter told me a math puzzle he had been working on. I was hopeless in math. I couldn't understand a word he was saying, but that didn't seem to matter. The puzzle was from a book of mathematical puzzles. He told me another.

The river was so dark, the stars reflected in it looked like they were hung in some second black sky. Looking down was so much like looking up that only the warmth of Carol's ankle in my hand gave me a sense of direction. I had no idea what time it was. Peter was on his fourth puzzle when the cops pulled up and shined a spotlight out over the water. Peter's voice died in midword. One of the cops called out, "Who's there?" I opened my mouth, but Carol answered, her voice clear and strong.

"Members of the Luna Heights Civic Association, Officer." A pause. The cop didn't answer. "We appreciate your concern." The spotlight snapped off, and the cruiser moved on. Peter and I pulled Carol up.

"Can you walk up to the house?" I asked. She nodded, then regretted it. We did get there eventually. Down the dock, up the stairs, the hill, our driveway, the steps to the front door. Peter left us there.

"I'm going to catch hell," he said, sounding both proud of himself and genuinely worried. "I'll call," he said to Carol.

After a stop at the bathroom, Carol and I made it down the hall to her bedroom. Her sweat smelled like Ripple, but she had stopped heaving. Now that she seemed mostly okay, I was mad at her.

I couldn't believe that after all she had said about how we didn't do things like that, she had gone and gotten drunk.

Our whole family, mother included, did do things like that. But I'd thought Carol meant just her and me, the two girls, the *real* family. Now she had given up on all her principles, just to get back a little popularity. At that moment, she seemed no different to me than Sergeant Nichols, the cop who had lectured us on bicycle safety in elementary school and on drugs in high school. He would hold up this tiny glass vial that was probably full of nothing but tap water and announce that it contained enough LSD to turn on the whole state of Florida. *Liars.*

"Thanks," Carol said when she was at last in bed, the covers up to her chin.

"I'm not sure I'm speaking to you," I said.

THE DAY AFTER *Oklahoma!* was Saturday. Carol was scheduled to have her wisdom teeth removed, something she'd refused to have done until the show was over. The oral surgeon had told my parents it would be easier to take out all four teeth at once and keep Carol in the hospital overnight. Carol was still hung over when she left with my father for the hospital, her skin a pale gray-green. If he noticed, my father probably thought it was makeup from the night before. When she came home on Sunday morning, she looked worse. She'd woken up in her hospital room after the surgery with her mouth packed full of bloody rolls of gauze.

Then the nurse brought in a tray of split pea soup and tomato juice. Just the sight of it, Carol said, had made her throw up.

She kept throwing up. She stayed home from school on Monday. Peter called, but she told me to say she was too sick to go to the phone. On Wednesday my father called our family doctor, Dr. Bach, who was giving my mother the Valium, and he called in a prescription for an antinausea drug for Carol. The blue station wagon brought it from Peebles Drugs along with my mother's weekly refill. After she took the medicine, Carol complained more, not less. Her legs kept cramping. Her tongue felt funny. She missed the rest of the week at school. I thought she was overdoing it, afraid to see any of her friends after *Oklahoma!,* or Peter after her night on the dock. I also thought she was trying to get my attention. I didn't want to forgive her just yet. I wanted to get even.

So I went to see Mark Lish. Mark had been one of my best friends in sixth grade. Back then, he, Marly Boggs, Joanna Fosbleck, and I were nearly inseparable. This was another case of the blindness of love. Honestly, I used to think *Joanna Fosbleck* was the most beautiful name in the world. How it rolled off the tongue! Jo-*ann*-a Fos-*bleck*. She moved away at the end of sixth grade. Mark, Marly, and I went on to junior high. My first day there, the day I embarrassed myself holding Marly's hand, I turned and saw Mark with new eyes. He was fat and his voice was still childishly high. I left a note in his locker saying maybe it would be better if we didn't see each other for a while. I knew it was a shitty thing to do, but I felt I had no choice.

Mark had gone on to become popular in his own way. By this time, he was widely reputed to be the biggest drug dealer in high school. Actually, he wasn't. His little brother Dana was, but it was a family business. Mark lived in Indian Heights, where most of the houses didn't have central air. Friday after school, I walked over there, crossed his yard, brown and full of sand spurs.

His mother was coming out. She was a short, dark-haired woman who worked at the public library. "Jesse," she said, stopping in the doorway, looking at me. "We haven't seen you in a while." I nodded, not sure whether she meant since she had seen me at the library or with Mark. Both were true. "Go on in." She held the screen door for me. "Mark's in the family room."

Mark was tall now, without an ounce of fat. He was sitting on the couch with his feet up on the coffee table, watching *Star Trek* and drinking from a quart bottle of Tab. He looked up. All the way over, I had been rehearsing my apologies and also trying to think of how to get around to what I wanted. Mark did not act surprised to see me. "Hey, kiddo," he said.

"Hey," I said back and sat down. He handed me a huge bowl of potato sticks.

After a few minutes, while Kirk and a landing party beamed down to yet another planet with an odd-colored sky, Mark got a box from under the couch and rolled a couple of joints. He lit one. I watched as he seemed to swallow the smoke and hold it. He handed me the roach clip, and I tried to do the same, but I coughed. Some of the smoke came out my nose. It was surprisingly hot. Mark handed me his Tab. He took another hit, and then I tried again. We passed the joint back and forth, until it was no more than a hot red point of light. Mark finished it. I felt nothing. Then I realized I had been breaking a single salty potato stick into smaller and smaller and smaller pieces for I didn't know how long. I ate it. Then stick by stick, I ate the whole bowl.

I looked up to see Captain Kirk standing, legs spread, hands on his hips under a bright purple sky. "Humans are not happy living in comfort," he said or something like that. "We *must* suffer. We like it." I nodded. It seemed obvious.

"Come on." Mark took me by the hand. He put a motorcycle helmet on my head, pulled the strap under my chin. Outside, he got on his bike.

I had never been on a motorcycle before. Basically, I was the kind of kid who, when I saw a ball coming, instead of trying to catch it, covered my face. I got on behind him. Mark told me to put my arms around his waist and hold on, so I did. Then we were off, and I closed my eyes against the wind. I felt the warmth of Mark's body through his T-shirt on my arms and my cheek. I felt the vibration of the bike, the way the cool air flowed out of the shade when we rode past a clump of trees. Even with my eyes shut, I knew we were on the River Road. Narrow, curving, dangerous. We flew down it, the wheels leaving the ground when we hit a bump. I smelled car exhaust and the river and the detergent Mark's mother used, and I had never been so happy. I felt paralyzed with joy.

We left the River Road, headed into Empire Heights, an unfinished subdivision. Up empty paved streets, past half-dead orange trees. This had been our secret playground when we were friends. Mark left the street and tore right up the tallest hill, the knobby tires of his bike spraying sand. At the top, he laid the bike on its side, having warned me to lift my leg. We rolled off and found ourselves in a hollow, all that was left of our old sand fort. We lay side by side, but not touching. My body missed his warmth, but Mark made no move to touch me. I was incapable of moving, numb. We smoked another joint.

Mark said he had decided to become a nuclear physicist. It took hard work and years of study but would be worth it. Then he told me that his father had been laid off at the Cape. We both knew that this was the beginning of the end.

Soon whole companies would be shutting down. The race for the moon was over. We had won. NASA had plans to rig up unused Apollo spacecraft into Skylab, a sort of temporary space station, but the flights to the moon were over. It was too expensive. Mark's father had once stayed awake for a solid seventy-two hours, working on the team that brought the crew of the disastrous Apollo 13 mission safely back to the earth. How could he sleep, he'd told Mark, when every minute Lovell and Swigert and Haise had less oxygen to breath? Now Mark's father had taken what he hoped would be a temporary job as a toll taker on the Bee Line Highway. Looked at in this light, it seemed good that Mark was on his way to becoming independently wealthy as a drug dealer. He would be able to pay his own way through college.

We got back on the motorcycle. After too short a time, Mark pulled up in front of my house. I got off, my legs unsteady. I took off the helmet and he strapped it on the back of the bike. Mark looked at me. I thought he was going to say something like, If you need me, you know where to find me. But he didn't say anything, and then he roared away. I stood in the hot sun on my driveway, my hair in my eyes. I tried to run my hand through it, but the hair was so tangled that my fingers got nowhere. Now I was ready to talk to Carol. I brushed the sand off my legs and went inside.

It was dark and cool, as always, but not quiet this time. My parents were in the kitchen arguing.

"I don't want to call Dr. Bach's service again!" my mother was saying. She sounded like she had been crying. "You don't know what it's like. I call and I call. He ignores me."

"But this isn't for you. Didn't you say it was about Carol?" my father said. I slammed the front door, coughed.

"Jesse!" I heard Carol calling, but her voice sounded strange, like her head was under the covers. "Jes, please." I walked down the hall and opened her door. What I saw was so strange that I thought it couldn't be real. I shook my head. It didn't go away. Carol was lying on her bed, but her back was impossibly arched, her face twisted. Only the tip of her head and her heels were touching the mattress. Even from across the room, I could smell her sweat and her fear. She was having some kind of convulsion.

"God," I said, running to her. I tried to push her down on the bed. How could I have doubted her when she told me how bad she felt?

"Please," she hissed between clenched teeth. "Get me out of here." Get me out of here. Out of this house, this family. I felt ashamed. Even Carol had given up on us.

I ran to the phone and called an ambulance, using a number from the orange emergency sticker on the receiver. My parents were still arguing like children: "You call." "No, you call." I wanted to scream at them. Instead, I just told them what I had done. By the time the ambulance attendants arrived, Mom and Dad were grown-up again. They acted like parents, asked questions. An attendant said the muscle seizures might be an allergic reaction to Compazine, the antinausea drug. A pretty common one. Allergic reaction, I thought, of course. Carol was allergic to everything. "Is she going to die?" I asked. I said this so they would say, Heavens no!

Instead one of them said, "It's best not to think about that right now." They put an oxygen mask on Carol, shot something into her arm. She relaxed a little and turned her head away from my parents. She looked at me. I leaned closer, and she said something I couldn't quite catch.

"Mmmm . . . nnn . . . mad at you" was what it sounded like. *Am* mad at you? Am *not* mad at you? Either way, I was sure she knew everything. She was either blaming me or forgiving me for what I had been doing all afternoon.

My parents climbed into the back of the ambulance with Carol, serious, adult, my mother clutching her purse. The last things I saw before they closed the backdoors were Carol's toes. As the ambulance started down the driveway, I realized I had no way to get to the hospital. I ran after it, hoping one of the attendants would see me in the rearview mirror and let me sit between them on the front seat. Instead, the driver hit the siren and was gone. I stopped at the end of the drive, breathing hard.

Just then a sheriff's car passed, stopped, backed up, and a deputy got out, hitching his belt. At once I was aware of my matted hair, my sandy clothes, which might or might not smell like pot.

"So," he said. "Somebody here OD'd?" He said the ambulance crew had called in a drug-related incident.

At first, I was so furious I couldn't say anything. Then I did. In a torrent. It wasn't an overdose, I said. My sister would never do anything like that. It was an allergic reaction to a drug our family doctor had prescribed. The deputy nodded patiently, and I realized that he had heard all of this many times before. My mother, full of legally prescribed Valium, could have been unconscious in that ambulance. Or Mark could have OD'd. Or me. It was all the same to him.

I accepted the deputy's offer of a ride to the hospital, but I couldn't shut up. I told him how when we were little, Carol would get so mad at me for reading all the time that she would tear the book from my hands. How I would just pick up another book and then another, until she would fall on me, punching me, pulling my hair. "She wanted me to play with her," I said. He nodded without taking his eyes from the traffic. " 'Look at me,' she used to say," I told him. "She wants people to *be* there when they're there."

"Yeah," he said, "well." He shrugged.

He dropped me off at the emergency entrance. I saw my parents on the far side of the waiting room, standing closer together than I could ever remember seeing them. I was walking toward them when the double doors next to them swung open and a doctor in green surgical scrubs stepped out. My parents turned their backs to me, their faces to him. I strained to hear what he was saying, but he was too far away. But I knew.

He had to be saying that Carol was dead.

The doctor's inaudible words seemed to roll like a wave across the room, washing over my mother and my father. I saw my mother's hands rise, my father's head snap back. Tonight my mother will throw her Valium down the garbage disposal, grind even the plastic bottle to bits. From now on, my father will come home every day at five. I will hug my mother and listen to my father. We will take up gardening or découpage or Chinese cooking, some hobby we all can share. The three of us will eat every meal together. It is not too late. We will be a family for Carol.

I braced myself, waiting for the wave to hit me. Instead, I heard my father's irritated voice. "I told you she would be fine," he said to my mother.

Carol was not dead.

I took a deep breath, prepared to feel joy or at least profound relief. Mostly I felt strange. Like I didn't know these people. Like this wasn't my family at all.

19

After Carol almost died, something happened to me. I disappeared inside my own body. I had the sensation of walking around and looking at my feet and my hands as if they were only remotely connected to anything I would call myself. Like I'd become the spaceship I'd fantasized I was when I'd been in my aluminum back brace. If I started to feel anything too keenly, I would close my eyes and build a capsule inside my head, sheet by heavy sheet. Sliding first the back wall in place, then the front, the sides, the top, cutting off all connections. Feeling the thick metal slice through brain and nerve and the tangled knots of worry. When I slid the bottom sheet in place, the part of me that was really me was deep inside a cold, quiet steel safe. Nothing could get to me at all.

Carol, even as distanced from the family as she was after what had happened, got worried about me. She went to my father and told him I was very unhappy. When he repeated her words to me, I was surprised. I didn't feel unhappy. I felt tired. Making a body that had so little to do with me get up every day, walk to the bus stop, and go to high school required concentrated effort. I came home each day and took long naps. Each night, I barely lasted through dinner, went to bed early. Still the alarm clock rang too soon. All I really wanted was to stay in bed and sleep forever, though it scared me to have this in common with my mother. My father talked to someone. I don't know who, maybe someone at the college who had trouble with their own kids. They recommended taking me to see a counselor at the local mental health center.

My father took off from work to take me, and I got to skip school as well. He was very nervous and talked nonstop about stuff in the news, Vietnam and Nixon, as we drove to my appointment at the center in Rockledge, the adjoining town. A fountain was in the courtyard outside the clinic. I remembered how my mother used to run water in the sink to get Carol and me to pee before we went on a long car trip or when we were supposed to fill up some little paper cup in the doctor's office for tests. I said to him, "Boy, I couldn't work here. The sound of that water would send me to the bathroom a thousand times a day." We both laughed, though it wasn't really all that funny.

After one talk with a woman counselor—she made me draw a picture of my family with crayons—I got assigned to group therapy. If I could come in on Mondays and Wednesdays, she said, I could join an ongoing group, one especially for teens in crisis. At the Cape, thousands of dads were being laid off. Houses were being repossessed, families coming apart. I wasn't surprised that other kids besides me were in trouble.

The first time that I went, the group leader, a thin, tall man with long brown hair pulled back in a ponytail, talked to me before the others came. He stood me in front of a full-length mirror. I'd let my own hair grow by then. My mother always liked it short, but now it was a regular blond bush, standing out from my head in a frizzy tangle. The counselor gathered it in his hands, holding it tight at the back of my neck. He asked me to look at myself. "Do you like your hair?" he asked, looking into my eyes reflected in the mirror.

"Sure," I said. I actually did like my hair. Even in my detached state, I considered it my best feature.

"Your forehead?" I nodded. He went on. "Your nose? Your mouth?"

I kept saying, yeah, sure, I liked all of them just fine. My body, that had so little to do with me, was just standing there in the mirror, looking back at me.

"Your breasts?" he asked. "Your vulva? Your vagina?"

I looked at him and thought, *What the hell does he want?* "Fine," I said to him, "I like my vagina just fine."

When he asked me how I liked my feet—my toes-out duck feet—my detachment finally broke down. I felt a rush of sympathy, sympathy I had refused to feel for myself. Poor feet. They'd had a hard life and deserved better.

The other kids started filing in. I was relieved to see I didn't know any of them, but I could tell from their clothes that these were cooler kids than me. Their jeans were more ragged, their bell-bottoms more extreme. One girl had a rose with a dagger through it tattooed above her skinny elbow. We sat on the floor in a circle and took turns talking. Most had been busted for drugs or shoplifting or running away from home. The group was a lesson in how to really mess up. One kid told how easy it was to hot-wire a car. Another about skipping school to do hash oil and break into his neighbors' houses. Their stories only made me feel more distant, even weirder. I'd been a saint compared to them. Me, I'd only smoked pot that one time with Mark Lish to get even with my sister. I'd never even thought of doing most of this stuff. It was embarrassing. I didn't talk at all that first meeting. Then, I started to lie.

One week, I said I'd stolen money from my mother's purse and also Valium from her medicine cabinet, which I'd sold in the girl's bathroom at my high school. Everybody nodded. I could tell they were starting to like me. I wasn't a stuck-up bitch after all. I'd just been a little shy. At the break, one kid tried to buy some Valium off me. When I said I didn't have any just then, she offered to sell me speed. The next week, I said I was in love with one of my teachers, that he'd kissed me. The counselor seemed to approve of that.

I started lying other places, too. I had a job at the public library, working a few hours after school repairing torn books, and there I practiced telling the older women working in the backroom the most outrageous things I could think of. I said my aunt was Jackie Kennedy Onassis. I brought in Carol's autographed picture of JFK as proof. I said next year I wouldn't be living in Cocoa, that I was going to Israel to live on a kibbutz with Golda Meir. I said this because, though I wasn't Jewish, I'd been the Israeli delegate at my high school's mock United Nations.

I told these lies as I worked, cutting huge sheets of cardboard into smaller pieces for the other women to stick inside broken bindings. One day I was so wrapped up in some complete fiction that I cut three fingernails off my left hand with the giant blade of the board shear. Another quarter inch and I would have lost the tops of half my fingers.

Then one week at group therapy, when everybody was just sitting there, at a loss for anything left in their short lives to confess, I told the group my mother had tried to kill herself. As soon as I said it, everyone sat up. I was surprised to find I was crying. I don't remember how I said she'd tried to do it, but while I talked I remember feeling sick, as if I were breaking some horrible taboo. I was afraid of bringing bad luck on my mother, that just telling such a lie might make it true. I thought I had finally gone unforgivably too far. Looking back now, I think I felt sick because it was true. She *was* killing herself. It was just taking years instead of minutes, like watching a terrible train wreck in slow motion.

After two months, I quit going to group. On the positive side, I came to the decision I didn't want to follow my group-mates into a life of boosting cars or eight-track tapes. On the negative, I just didn't want to talk about how I felt anymore. Whatever was happening to me was something I more than deserved. It was only fair that all my years of lying had led to my loss of self.

What I wanted, instead, was out. Out of school, out of the house, out of everything that had made up my life until then. One day, standing outside the school cafeteria, dreading going back to English class to diagram more sentences, I saw a way. Because I'd heard my father talk about it, I knew that the courts had struck down the requirement that girls in

Florida public schools take a year of home ec and the boys, a year of shop. The number of hours required to graduate from high school was actually pretty low. Most kids took lots of electives, band or typing or, like my sister, chorus. The bottom line was three years of English, two years of math, two of science, two of PE, and a semester of something called Americanism Versus Communism, designed to convince us how lousy it would be to live in the Soviet Union. This was an entire term of filmstrips where they did things like show a giant shoe store in America as a deep voice said, "In America, we have a choice of shoes, but in Russia"—bring up the heavy Volga Boatmen music, fade-in a shot of one ugly pair of granny boots—"choice is not allowed."

Kids who flunked or who wanted to take even more electives during the day signed up for night school. An eight-week course at night carried a year's credit. Nasty requirements could be quickly gotten out of the way. I had no hobbies, so I'd already taken most of what I needed to graduate. I was only short one credit in English and one in PE, which I'd been putting off because I hated it so much. If I went to night school, I could graduate a year early.

As soon as I had the idea, I started to have doubts. I'd miss my senior year, prom and all, which everyone said was important, not that high school had been my favorite thing so far in life. I was a big fan of an old show on TV called *The Prisoner* about an ex-spy locked up on an island resort that was actually a prison. On that show, whenever anybody said good-bye to anyone else on the island, they'd always say, "Be seeing you," a remark that I found wonderfully ironic. Of course, they would be seeing one another because there was no escape from the island, though the imprisoned spy tried every week. It was the way I thought of school, the way I thought of my whole life. In the last episode, the prisoner did escape, blowing the island apart behind him.

When I got home from school that day, my mother was awake and sitting on the couch. By then, she was really in bad shape. On those nights when she came to dinner, she often choked on her food. Tea or bread would run from her mouth and nose right onto her plate. When Carol or I asked my father about her, he just repeated her doctor's line about how she would be much worse without the medication. How? I should have asked. How could she possibly have been worse?

Now, of course, after Betty Ford and the experiences of a thousand other women, I can see it was the Valium that was killing her. Instead of helping, the Valium only made her more and more depressed. Her doctor gave it to her, gave her more and more, because that was what doctors were told to do for women who took to their beds but didn't sleep, who were unhappy without knowing why. On top of everything else, the summer before, she'd had a mastectomy. This was in the days when women routinely went in to have a lump checked and woke up with half their chests missing. I'd been away at the time. My father had sent me to visit my half-sister Bobbie, a trip that was probably another of Carol's ideas to cheer me up. No one told me about the surgery until I got back. Carol, who was driving by then, picked me up at the airport.

"She came through the surgery okay," she said, "but it was cancer." She shook her head, very adult and in charge. Then later, as we drove across the swampy basin of the St. John's River, she said, "You know, at the hospital Dad and I got talking." She looked at me sideways, driving fast. "We both agreed it might be best for everybody if Mom just didn't make it." I stared at her. What she said was horrible, and we both knew it. But by this time Carol wanted out as badly as I did, as we all did. We'd turned into some kind of emotional Donner party. Wishing our mother dead was just one more little thing we were willing to do in the name of our survival.

Mom did make it. As soon as I saw her in the hospital, I knew I didn't want her to die. She was my mother, and I loved her. The surgery actually pulled her together—she was always good in an emergency—and for a few months she became once again the mother who could drive a car with one hand and smoke and tell great Women's Army Corps stories all at the same time. I would have died for her.

So the day I conceived my plan, I sat down in the chair next to the couch and talked to Mom about this and that, like the old days. She sat there, listening, nodding. I thought about Carol's friend Stephanie, who couldn't believe I didn't tell my mother everything. So I said, "Mom, I'm thinking about graduating from school a year early. But I don't know. What do you think?" My chest felt cramped with the importance of what I was asking. My whole life, it seemed, would be decided by whether or not I did this.

My mother looked at me for a very long time. I thought maybe she hadn't really heard me. I opened my mouth to repeat what I'd said, but before I could, she answered.

"Why should I care?" she said and closed her eyes.

In a real way, I deserved that answer. I wasn't actually asking her advice. I would do what I wanted. I was the one who had said nothing when my sister told me we would be better off with our mother dead, the one who hadn't asked nearly enough questions about why and how my mother had gotten to be the mess she was. None of us had. As a family, we all deserved that answer from my mother.

In another way, her answer was truly terrible. From my brief spell in a Methodist Sunday school, I remember a discussion of just which sin it was that the Bible called "the sin that cannot be forgiven." Maybe this was it. I was just a kid, and no kid deserves to have her mother stop caring. I felt like someone had punched me in the chest. I stood up from the chair across from her, walked down the hall to the bathroom, and threw up.

I went to night school. I must have gotten my father's permission to do it, but I don't remember. My English class was full of girls so pregnant they had to sit sideways because there wasn't room for their stomachs in the small school desks. Even though these girls were in my high school, or had been, I didn't know any of them. It made me realize what a little pool—"We're Advanced"—I had been swimming in. The teacher was a young black woman. The official policy for night school was that we did all our writing in class, no homework. Maybe to forestall cheating, maybe to make sure we did it. The other girls took a lot of time to complete the simplest assignment, some because they weren't trying, most because they could barely read or write. The teacher and I would sit at the front and talk about books we'd read.

She was waiting to get called up for officers' training in the Marines. The war in Vietnam was almost over, so she didn't think she'd get sent there. She wanted something better than teaching. I liked her more than any teacher I had ever had, maybe because she reminded me of what my mother must have been like in the WACs. After I finished her course, she did get called up. She sent me a postcard from Camp Pendleton with a picture of her barracks on it.

I also took night PE, a scary class where the boys were all guys who'd gotten kicked out of day PE for punching the coach or knifing a fellow student. We played volleyball in the middle of the gym. An off-duty cop had been hired to keep score.

By the end of my junior year, I had exactly enough credits to graduate. My principal was still Mr. Trumbell, the one who looked like Gus Grissom. He had been promoted from the junior high to the high school. When I told him what I was planning, he buzzed his secretary and demanded she bring in my cumulative folder. Then he slammed his finger in his desk drawer while going for a pencil. He was that angry.

He was afraid he'd lose half the student body if word of what I'd done got around. He'd been a principal long enough to know that no matter how much fun high school appeared to be in the movies or on TV, not too many students would volunteer for an extra year of it. I just sat in front of him with my legs and my fingers crossed. Mr. Trumbell looked long and hard at that manila-clad record of my transgressions and grades. Then he sighed.

"Well, it doesn't look like I have much choice. I'll sign off on this. But I won't just let you jump willy-nilly into the senior class," Mr. Trumbell said, his eyebrows dark and drawn. Therefore I would not be allowed to take part in graduation, in the ceremony in which my sister Carol would be finishing with honors. They would send me my diploma in the mail.

I didn't give a damn. I was euphoric. I was in a fast car racing toward the future, in a rocket that was blasting off, the earth below me nothing but a deep blue marble. The universe would be my infinite new home. I was sixteen.

"Be seeing you," I said. I was out of there.

20 January 1974

"What would you give to know the meaning of life?"

I was sitting in the darkened multitorium in the middle of my World Religion class. I'd escaped high school, but I had only gotten as far as my father's junior college. Usually we spent both hours of World Religion in the dark, watching a psychedelic swirl of slides flashing from six projectors onto three screens, listening to chants of the world booming from the tall black speakers that flanked them. Our teacher, Dr. Lauden, lived in a Winnebago camper in the school's parking lot. He had once been a Methodist minister, but now he had bigger ideas.

"To know the one secret necessary to understand your place in the cosmos. What would you give?" Dr. Lauden prodded us. He was sitting on the edge of the stage, dressed in worn bell-bottoms and a flamingo pink shirt. He swung his feet back and forth over the orchestra pit, staring out at the darkness that held the fifty or so students in the class. Some were taking the class for the third or fourth time, even though they could only get credit for it once. "Would you give your most precious worldly possession?"

I leaned forward in my seat. What would I give? I wanted to know the answer. I *needed* to know. I thought about the gold pocket watch hooked inside my macramé purse. I'd bought it for myself as a graduation gift when it became clear my parents had no thought of giving me anything. Marly's parents had given her a pair of fourteen-carat-gold earrings, Lynn's, a typewriter and a college dictionary. In my family, graduating was a given, not worthy of any particular celebration. We were just supposed to do it from time to time, like brushing our teeth or washing our hair. I gazed up at Dr. Lauden and imagined laying my precious watch at his feet, or at least on the stage next to him.

"Why don't you just tell us, Doc?" a kid to the left of me called out.

"I could, but then it wouldn't mean anything. Knowledge is worthless without sacrifice," Dr. Lauden said. "This weekend I fasted, Saturday to Sunday, nothing but bread and water. Early this morning, I walked to the grocery store and bought an orange. Just the smell of that orange in my hand was heaven. When I tore open the skin . . ." Dr. Lauden took a deep breath and spread his arms. *"Ecstasy!"* He smiled at us. "So I am asking. What would you give to know the truth?"

I had a vision of myself on my knees like some medieval pilgrim creeping over the great arched span of the bridge to Cape Kennedy. I closed my eyes and imagined the scrape, scrape, scrape of my jeans on the concrete. It would be hard, but for once I would have a real purpose.

"Ah, well," Dr. Lauden said, interrupting my mental pilgrimage. "I don't want to be unfair. I'll tell you. The secret is this." He paused a long time. No one made a sound. "You were never born. And . . . you will never die."

I could feel the disappointment around me in the dimness. What did that mean? Never born? Never die? Our births were something we took for granted. At seventeen or eighteen, our deaths something too distant to concern us. It was what to do next, after this class, after these two years in junior college, that was the impossible burden.

Then I remembered that I had met Dr. Lauden years before at a party Carol and I had gone to with my parents when we first moved to Cocoa. He had a house on the beach then, complete with a widow's walk and a yard full of sea oats and sand dunes. He was married, too. Did I remember someone saying it was his wife's house? Carol and I ran barefoot on the beach with his three blond, sunburned sons and the children of some of the other guests, pretending we were wild mustangs. When it was dark and time to go in, Dr. Lauden called his boys over to introduce them to the other parents. "This is David," he said, saying the oldest boy's name but motioning to Charlie, the youngest, who was eight. "He's six." He went on, introducing each son in some mangled way, too drunk or stoned or just plain absent-minded to remember his own children's ages and names. Where were his sons now? Did they think he was wise? Was he their guru?

After a brief reprise of Javanese gamelan music, one of Dr. Lauden's favorite tapes, the class was over. I gathered up my books and headed for anthropology, which was at the other end of the campus. After the dark of the multitorium, my eyes watered in the afternoon sun. "He's lost his faith," someone said to me. I blinked in the general direction of the voice and recognized the outline of a fellow World Religion student, Rafe Rivard, a big guy, well over six feet, with long brown hair. He always seemed to choose the seat directly behind me. Standing next to him, I felt like a toy poodle at the feet of a bull mastiff.

"You mean Dr. Lauden?" I said. Rafe nodded. Considering Dr. Lauden's evenhanded praise for the Buddha, Mohammed, Jesus, Moses, and Martin Luther King, I wondered which faith Rafe was talking about. Then my eyes adjusted to the sunlight and took in the cross Rafe was wearing. It hung from his neck on a worn leather bootlace and looked for all the world like two miniature railroad spikes welded together.

"These other religions have lessons to teach us, of course," Rafe said, "but there is no sense in pretending that we can reach God without going through Jesus." Rafe shifted his books from one large arm to the other. I noticed he was taking anthropology, too. "Christianity is our heritage."

"Hmmm," I said. I was technically, if not enthusiastically, a Christian. For two brief months, Carol had had a crush on Tad Gentry, who attended the First Methodist Church and even MYF, Methodist Youth Fellowship. She'd gotten me to go to church with her so she could sit a few rows behind him and gawk. Having had no instruction in the existence or nonexistence of God whatsoever, Carol had unexpectedly decided to take it all very seriously. One Easter Sunday, Carol and I had been simultaneously baptized and confirmed into the Methodist Church.

All I really remembered was that the minister, making his way with cupped palms down the row of bent heads, baptized each with a sprinkle of water. Reaching me last, he opened both hands and dumped what seemed like a pint of cold water down the back of my neck. I took my first communion (a cube of white bread, carefully trimmed of crust, and a little thimble of grape juice) with water dripping from my hair and chin and running under the white collar of my baptismal robe. After all that, Carol decided to unconvert, to dislike Tad, and to become a serious atheist.

"Can I walk with you to class?" Rafe asked.

"Sure," I said, fighting an impulse to say no and bolt. It wasn't so much that Rafe, grim cross and all, scared me, as that I didn't want to know anyone in my classes. That was the glorious freedom of junior college; no one knew me. After living ten years in Cocoa, everyone in high school knew exactly who I was. I couldn't escape their conception of me. Now I could be anyone, if I could just figure out who I wanted to be.

As we walked across the middle of the flat, treeless campus my father had helped design, Rafe revealed that he planned to attend seminary and become a Methodist minister, one who would not lose his faith the way Dr. Lauden had. He told me he planned to become a missionary and serve God all his days. We reached class just as he finished telling about a vision his mother had had of his being one of the chosen of God. This didn't sound all that odd to me. *Time* and *Newsweek* were full of stories about the Jesus people, Freaks for Jesus, ex-hippies who, having tried drugs and meditation and Marx, were returning in droves to Christianity, their parents' faith, but in a slightly groovier, up-to-date form. Rafe, in his shoulder-length hair and handmade leather sandals, looked the part.

We climbed the stairs to the second floor of the social sciences building, stopped outside our classroom. "I have a confession to make," Rafe said, as if what he had told me before was mere chitchat. "When I walked into World Religion, the first thing I saw was you, your blond hair shining in the darkness." Rafe looked down at me. I noticed his eyes were blue, as pale and pure as bottled water. "I kept sitting behind you, trying to get up my courage, but I thought a girl like you wouldn't want to talk to me."

A girl like me? What kind of girl did he think I was? Rafe sighed deeply, and as if I could read his mind, I saw myself as he saw me: blond, bird-boned, tiny compared to him. He was certain I'd been popular in high school, a cheerleader or even a homecoming queen. I'd always had my pick of boys and would never talk to someone like him. He didn't know that my only boyfriend had asked for his name bracelet back a week after he'd given it to me. This happened one day at lunch in front of everybody we knew. Rafe didn't know I'd had to beg a friend to take me to the junior prom. He thought I was cute, sexy even. I saw an all-new me reflected in his eyes.

"Do you think," Rafe said, twisting his cross on its leather thong, "you might like to go to a movie this weekend? If you aren't busy?"

The reading in our anthropology text that week had been about a tribe in the Amazon who communicated through an elaborate sign language. If one Indian met another stronger and superior to himself on a path in the jungle, the first would show he did not wish to fight by beating the outside of his thighs, clearly signaling, our text said, *I am already subdued. You do not need to subdue me.* When Rafe asked me out, I had a strong impulse to beat the outside of my thighs. "Sure," I said, "if there's something good on."

Rafe picked me up in his car, a green '68 Plymouth Fury that was jacked up in the back like a drag racer and had valves that rattled like old bones whenever Rafe stepped on the gas. He'd bought the car, he told me, with the money he made working the night shift at a plant outside town that made electronic circuits for B-1 bombers. The company had just moved the plant to Cocoa from California to take advantage of all the laid-off Cape workers. Cheap labor, Rafe explained.

We went to see *Towering Inferno* at the big new mall on Merritt Island, spending two and a half hours trying to guess which stars would burn to death, which would survive. Since there was hardly a building tall enough to need an elevator in Brevard County, the threat of death in a hundred-story high-rise was hard to take seriously, but the idea of dying by fire reminded me of Gus Grissom and Apollo 1. When we left the theater, I felt shaky, like I'd been watching a real disaster in Cinemascope.

Rafe's engine rattled its way back over the humped causeway. He had to be at his job by midnight, he said. We got back to Luna Heights at eleven, and Rafe circled the block. My house looked dark, but since the family room was in the back, those lights didn't show from the street. I couldn't tell if my father was home watching TV or still at the office. My mother, I was sure, was in bed.

Carol was away at college, living in a red brick dorm in Tallahassee. She'd done volunteer work during her senior year in high school with retarded kids at the training center in town, helping them découpage pictures from magazines onto empty lard cans to sell as decorative trash cans. She had fallen in love with them. They deserved help, she'd said at dinner one night, because they always tried their best. I thought she was implying that she couldn't say the same about us, her family. All she could talk about was going to Florida State University, six hours away in north Florida, to get her degree in special education. In the fall, she'd gone.

Now she was interning at Sunland, a residential center for profoundly retarded adults. Her phone conversations were full of talk of catheters and feeding tubes and the value of playing music on the wards. Her voice burned with dedication. She'd had to go a long way to find a group more helpless than our family to care for, but she had done it. I hoped they realized how lucky they were to have her.

Rafe circled the block again. I realized he was waiting for instructions. "You can park on the street," I said. "We don't have to go in." He pulled the car up to the curb in front of the Boggses' house, and we sat in the dark listening to the mosquitoes hum, the frogs singing in the orange trees. Marly Boggs had joined the air force, was off somewhere learning to repair radar. Her father still had his job at the Cape but fully expected to be laid off any day.

I kept looking across the street at my house. I wasn't nervous that Mom or Dad would wonder where I could be. It was just that the house looked so dead from the street, like a big family tomb. This was the view Mrs. Boggs and our other neighbors had had of us for years: dead house, dying family.

Rafe coughed. "I'm sorry," I said, shaking my head. I didn't want to tell him about my family, about anything. I wanted to stay Rafe's mystery girl as long as possible. "I've just got a lot on my mind."

Rafe took my hand. He told me he could feel I had troubles. Who didn't? But if I let Jesus into my life, if I just closed

my eyes and said, Help me, Lord, then He would take control of my life and find the path that was truly right for me.
Jesus would take my heart in his hands and never let go.

I closed my eyes, got as far as *help*. "Please," I said to God
or somebody. I *was* lost. I did want to be found. I felt something wet on my cheek. I was crying.

Rafe kissed me, his lips soft on my wet cheek. I kissed him
back. His mouth was wide; even his teeth were oversized.
His hand was so large it covered half my chest. Under his
palm, I could feel my heart pounding. We kissed until my
lips were raw, until my teeth hurt, until the car windows
were completely fogged and dripping. Sometime later, I
heard the jangling of the tags on Bertha's collar. My father
was walking her around the block. Bertha was our only pet
now. Lucky had died the year before, his kidneys finally giving out. My mother had become hysterical at the news, crying uncontrollably, as if this small cat death were the one
thing she couldn't bear. I froze as the jangling tags came
closer. My father didn't know what Rafe's car looked like,
but in our neighborhood, with its wide drives and two-car
garages, no one parked on the street. Surely, he would be curious, take a look.

"Shhh," I said to Rafe, "it's my father."

Rafe slumped down in the car seat, trying to become invisible, but his knee hit the eight-track player, pushed the

tape in, and suddenly "Stairway to Heaven" was blasting out of the speakers mounted under the rear window. Rafe jerked the tape out and threw it in the backseat.

"Come on, Bertie girl," I heard my father say in the silence that followed. Bertha sniffed at the Boggses' grass and moved on, my father in tow. I couldn't tell whether he had noticed us but had pretended not to or whether he was really and truly blind.

"Oh, God," Rafe said, his eyes closed as if this were a prayer.

"It's okay," I said, "really," and kissed him again.

I HAD HAD a luckier life than Rafe, even if I hadn't been anybody's homecoming queen. On our second date, Rafe said he wanted to take me by the house, maybe meet his mom. Rafe lived in Titusville, the town just north of Cocoa, with his mother, sister, stepfather, two stepbrothers, and two stepsisters. All eight were squeezed in a small three-bedroom house in a run-down subdivision, Hamlet Hills. Once a swamp, it was almost drained now. The streets were named after characters in Shakespeare's tragedy: Claudius Way, Laertes Lane, Hamlet Terrace. As we drove to Rafe's house, I couldn't help noticing there wasn't a street named after Horatio, the play's sole significant survivor. Rafe lived at 22 Ophelia Court, a dead end with a murky pond behind it. Were the street names meant ironically? Probably not. In Cocoa there was a subdivision, even more run-down and depressing, whose streets were named after Ivy League colleges. The paper was always full of arrests made on Harvard, Princeton, and Yale.

That first visit, we parked at the curb, crossed the brown yard, and entered through a jalousied front door that had so many panes missing it seemed silly that it had a knob and lock. Inside, the house smelled of mold, damp, and mildew. The only furniture in the living room was a couch with the legs broken off and an old TV missing its knobs. A girl about my age was asleep on the couch in a plaid pajama top and bikini underwear, though it was late afternoon. A boy about fourteen was changing channels with a pair of pliers.

"That's Lisa," Rafe said, pointing at the couch. Lisa was his sister. She opened one eye and waved. She had blue eyes and long dark hair like Rafe's. "And this is Lonnie." The boy with the pliers smiled. He was razor thin with short blond hair and looked nothing like Rafe. I figured he was either a stepbrother or a neighbor.

"I'll get us something to drink," Rafe said. I followed him into the kitchen. Lonnie was his youngest stepbrother and—Rafe lowered his voice—Lonnie was a bit slow. Rafe opened the refrigerator. Inside was a nearly empty bottle of catsup and a large jar of grape jam. I'd never seen a refrigerator that empty unless it was being defrosted, but Rafe did not seem surprised. "There's always water," he said. He got down two jelly-jar glasses with Flintstones cartoons on them and turned on the tap. The pipes knocked loudly, but not a drop of water came out.

"I'm running a bath," Lisa called from the living-room sofa.

"Low water pressure," Rafe explained. He set the jelly jars on the counter. "Come on, I'll show you around." He led me down the short central hall. The door to the bathroom was open, rusty water trickling from the faucet into the tub. At that rate, I thought, Lisa might be clean by dinner. I couldn't imagine how eight people got bathed and showered and shaved in that house in a month, let alone every day.

Rafe showed me his room, where all three boys slept, two in a bunk bed, one on a foldaway. Rafe had painted the walls red, white, and blue with stars and stripes, like an American flag. The three girls slept in a second, smaller bedroom. At the end of the hall was the door to his parents' room. It had a large dead bolt. Rafe knocked and said, "It's me, Mom."

"Just a minute." The lock went clunk, and Rafe opened the door. In the light of a large color TV, I caught my first glimpse of Mrs. Rivard, standing by the side of a king-size bed in a bright purple pants suit, putting on a pair of fluffy mules. She waved us in. I knew from what Rafe had said that his mother was forty, almost young enough to be my mother's daughter. What struck me was how much they looked alike. Soft, blank eyes, as if they had just woken up from a bad dream, gray hair overdue for a permanent. "Oh, honey," Mrs. Rivard kissed me, her lips soft and warm. "I'm so happy to meet you. Welcome to the family."

Next to the bed was a small refrigerator and on top of it a horde of stacked boxes of cookies and chips. Such a wealth of snack food was shocking after the bare kitchen outside. I thought of my mother, her perpetually closed door. Was this any different? It seemed to me it was, but I wasn't sure how. I stepped back, not wanting Mrs. Rivard to kiss me again. She opened her refrigerator. "Here, honey," she said, handing me a Coke. "You look thirsty."

All the kids had jobs, Rafe told me later, and were expected to buy food and clothes out of their earnings. Everyone worked. His mother was a secretary, his stepfather a county mosquito control officer during the day and a convenience store clerk at night. To Rafe, it wasn't odd that his mother kept her food and TV behind a locked door. If she didn't, someone would take them.

I found out what he meant. After we had been dating a month, I started to send Rafe home with packed lunches for his night job, raiding leftovers from my mother's cooking that none of us had much heart for. If he put his lunch in the refrigerator, one of his siblings would eat everything but the napkin, no matter how dire the threats he Magic Markered on the brown bag.

I felt rich sending food home with him, like I was from a better planet or a home where things really worked. That was part of Rafe's appeal. His family was so messed up and so open about it that I could pretend mine was just fine. In the time I knew him, both his stepsisters got pregnant. His stepfather threw the oldest one out in the yard with all her stuff in the middle of the night. Then her boyfriend retaliated by shooting out what was left of the jaulosies in the front door. Rafe's oldest brother got caught in bed by his girlfriend's father and so managed to get married and join the navy in a single day. The youngest brother, sweet, slow Lonnie, failed the test to join the army and went to live on the beach with an older man. Then he disappeared. He was never seen or heard from again. Rising above this chaos was Rafe — attending college, headed for seminary — the family's great hope, his mother's proof that life was worth living in spite of everything. I was added evidence. Since Rafe thought I was superior to him, his mother thought I was a princess. My choosing Rafe only proved her vision was true. Rafe was God's anointed, a true prince.

I was working, too. I had a job in the junior college's bookstore. I thought I'd gotten the job on my own, that no one—not the manager of the bookstore, Mrs. Janish, nor any of my teachers—knew who my father was. This in spite of the fact that he was now provost of the Cocoa campus, the biggest part of a junior college that had expanded to have campuses in Melbourne and Titusville as well. The bookstore employed five students, and except for the long lines of students waiting to buy textbooks at the beginning of the semester, we were never busy. The bookstore was in the student union, so we took turns running across the hall to buy Cokes and onion rings at the snack bar and to bring back reports on the Watergate hearings, which played day after day on the TV in the student lounge.

One morning I was working on the display case under the cash register, dusting the new electronic calculators for sale, each the size of a small typewriter, when I looked up to see Mrs. Janish pop out of her office. Something was wrong. She had both hands pressed to her lips. She looked like she might be sick. "What?" I started.

"Sit down," she said to me. She waited until I was perched on the high wooden stool we kept behind the counter. "The provost is in the hospital," she said. "He had a heart attack this morning in his office." At first I thought she was telling me this without knowing the provost was my father. Then she put her hand on my shoulder. "Your sister is at the hospital with him." Carol was home for spring break. "She wants you to stay here for now. She'll call." I had just gotten my driver's license, but I didn't have a car. I guessed I would stay where I was. Where was my mother?

"Did she say how my father is?" I couldn't imagine my father in the hospital. He had high blood pressure, I knew, but he didn't smoke or drink or even, as he had told so many waitresses over the years, drink coffee.

"She said they were running tests."

I finished dusting and rearranging the display case. Then, at Mrs. Janish's insistence, I went across the hall to get some lunch. My English professor, who was busy convincing an entire generation of Brevard County kids that Shakespeare was really Christopher Marlowe, stopped me. "I was so shocked and sorry to hear about your dad," he said. The woman at the grill who made the onion rings, each hand-sliced and dipped in fresh batter, said, "Such terrible news about your father." So much for anonymity.

After lunch, Carol called. "The doctors say the next twenty hours are the most important," she said. He had been feeling pain in his chest and left arm for several days but had ignored it. My father had brought home Kentucky Fried Chicken for dinner last night, something I couldn't re-member him ever doing before, and we'd eaten the whole bucket. Even my mother had a nice, juicy breast. It was hard to believe that instead of licking our fingers, we should have been dialing my father an ambulance, racing to the hospital.

"Listen, Carol," I said, "where's Mom? I can't stay here."

I heard her hesitate. "She's in with Dad, but I'm sending her home. She's not doing so well."

"Are you going home with her?" We both knew someone should stay with her. I knew neither of us wanted to.

"No," Carol said, "I'm staying with Dad." She was choosing sides. I would have to as well.

"I'll get a ride to the hospital," I said. "Rafe will be out of class in an hour. Or I'll get one of the other kids at the bookstore to take me."

"Come straight to intensive care," Carol said. "It's on the second floor."

In the end, Mrs. Janish volunteered to drive me to the hospital. We got there a little before two. "I hope your father's okay," she said, dropping me off outside the main lobby. "The college wouldn't be the same without him."

A sign to the right of the double doors that lead into Intensive Care read: IMMEDIATE FAMILY ONLY!!! FIVE-MINUTE LIMIT ON VISITS. CHECK-IN REQUIRED. STOP AT THE NURSING DESK. It wasn't a good sign that my father was in a place where such strict rules were necessary.

The nursing desk was just inside the double doors. I

stopped to check in as required, but the nurse held a finger to her lips. I mouthed my father's name. She nodded and pointed to one of the glass cubicles. He was resting, his eyes closed, breathing through a tube. Carol was sitting on a hard plastic chair by his side. She got up, her five minutes over, and let me have her place.

I leaned forward and took his hand in mine. It was very warm, the small bones moving slightly under a soft cushion of flesh. He didn't move. He was hooked up to a monitor, one of those machines that made each heartbeat into a game of follow the bouncing ball. The rhythm was insistent, hypnotic. His lips were purplish blue. After a while, I started to cry.

The nurse appeared at the cubicle door. She touched her watch with one finger. My five minutes were up. "He'll probably be livelier tomorrow," she said, and I couldn't help wondering if *livelier* was an intensive-care euphemism for *still alive*. She walked with me back to the double doors. "Right now, he's on some pretty heavy meds."

Carol was waiting for me in the lobby, sitting hunched on one of the bright orange plastic couches, her arms wrapped around her waist as if her stomach hurt. I sat beside her. She looked almost as bad as Dad.

Carol looked over at me. "I'm the reason for all this."

"What in the world are you talking about?"

"They had to get married because of me," Carol said, hugging her stomach even harder. "Mom told me last year. She was pregnant. The WACs offered her an abortion, but she wouldn't do it. She said Dad proposed by saying, 'Well, then I guess I'll have to marry you.'" Carol started crying. "It's all my fault. My fault, they had to get married, and now they're both sick and unhappy. I tried my best, but it wasn't enough."

"That's crazy," I told her. "We're the kids. We're not supposed to be in charge."

She looked up at me, one eyebrow raised, as if to say, *If not us, who?* Then she wiped her eyes with an already damp, wadded Kleenex and sighed. "Did I tell you Sanders broke up with me?" she said. Sanders was her latest boyfriend. He'd transferred to Cocoa High as a senior and taken Carol to the prom. I didn't like him much. When I'd represented Israel at the mock United Nations during my junior and final year in high school, Sanders had been the chief delegate from the Soviet Union. In the middle of a crucial debate about the Gaza Strip, the Palestinian observer had tried to abduct me from the women's rest room. I had barely escaped, after spending the better part of an hour locked in a stall. I had no doubt that the kidnapping stunt had been Sanders's idea. He was that kind of guy.

After graduation, he'd been one of the few kids in our

class to go to college out of state, to Duke. "You remember how I asked him to look up Deena Quinn, because she was at UNC and I thought she'd be lonely?" Deena had been the treasurer of the high school French Club, a position that guaranteed negative social stature. She was a smart, sweet girl with thick, black-framed glasses. "Well, he did, and now they're planning on moving out of their dorms next year and living together."

None of Carol's plans for the people she loved, who all should have loved her more, were working out. "Come on," I said, putting my arm around her. "Let's go get a Coke or something. Then I need to call Rafe."

21

We decided to take shifts. Carol would stay with Dad until dinnertime, then I would take a turn, bringing Mom with me if she was up to it. Rafe picked me up outside the hospital. I slid into the passenger seat of his car and almost sat on a half-dozen red roses. "For my dad?" I said, wondering if I should tell Rafe they didn't allow flowers in intensive care.

"For you," he said. "Come on. There's somewhere special—" he hesitated, "somewhere sacred, I want to take you." I didn't know what to say. I shut the door. I thought maybe we were going to see his minister, Dr. Bingen, to talk about my father. I'd met him the one Sunday I had gone to a service with Rafe. Rafe's Methodist church had been a congregation of United Brethren, a small, historically German-speaking denomination that had recently joined the much larger Methodists to form the United Methodist Church. I didn't know how a group of German Protestants had ended up in Titusville, but the members of Rafe's church were mostly elderly people with names like Wipperfurth and Schattschneider. They loved Rafe. Even though he wasn't in the least bit German, he was their future, proof that the generation to come was not wholly lost, wicked, or mad. The Sunday I'd gone to church, they'd smiled at me as if Rafe and I were the new Adam and Eve.

Rafe didn't head for the church, which was near Hamlet Hills. Instead he parked in downtown Titusville, in front of one of the many empty storefronts. "Where are we going?" I asked him, as we got out of the car. "I have to be back at the hospital by five."

"Don't worry, we will be," he said. "Now close your eyes." He put his hands over my eyes and steered me down a short flight of stairs. I heard a door open, a shop bell ring. I smelled damp and sawdust and something stronger, leather. "Okay," Rafe said, and lifted his hands. We were in a leather goods shop. Purses and bags made out of stiff, stitched cowhide hung on the walls. The back was curtained off by an Indian print bedspread, maybe to make space for a dressing room, maybe because someone lived back there. An old-fashioned pedal sewing machine took up the center of the room. Rafe picked up a sheet of paper and a thick carpenter's pencil from the counter.

"Here," he said and motioned me to a short stool. "Sit down and take off your shoes. I need to trace your foot."

"Why?" I asked.

"So your sandals will fit, silly," Rafe said. Then I understood, at least partly, why we were there. I'd said I liked Rafe's sandals. With their flat, thick soles and complicated leather laces, they looked like something the Roman legions or maybe Christ himself might have worn. Now I was about to be fitted for my own pair.

I sat down, slipped off my white plastic sandals. A short, bald man with a thick, black beard appeared from behind the curtain. "Joseph," Rafe announced, smiling. Joseph, the sandal-maker, wore blue-and-white-striped overalls but no shirt. A nail cross, identical to Rafe's, hung from a leather bootlace around his neck. Rafe nodded toward a display on the counter: a row of crosses swung from a wooden stand made of dowels. "Joseph's wife, Patience, makes the crosses." I tried to imagine someone named Patience who spent her days welding spikes into symbols of her Lord's martyrdom. *Patience.* Would I be a better person if my name were Harmony or Charity?

"Here," Joseph said to Rafe, taking the paper and pencil from him. "I'll do it." Joseph knelt beside me, lifted my

slightly dirty bare foot onto the paper. His fingers were calloused, so hard they felt like bare bones. I watched as he
carefully traced my left foot. Hanging half-tangled in his
dark, curling chest hair, the sharp ends of his cross looked
painful and dangerous.

"The first time I came in here," Rafe said, "I saw those
crosses and knew I wanted one. I didn't know why. I wasn't
a Christian then. I didn't have any money, so I waited until
Joseph went in the back, and I stole one." Rafe touched the
cross around his neck. "This one." I looked down at Joseph,
but he didn't seem to be listening. He was starting on my
right foot. "But I couldn't bring myself to wear it. I mean, it
bothered my conscience. So I brought it back. Patience was
working, and I told her what I'd done. She gave me a Bible.
You know, one of those little green Gideon New Testaments.
She told me to come back the next day to talk to Joseph."

Joseph looked up at Rafe and smiled. He had a beautiful
smile, full of really nice white teeth, but it only lasted a second. He touched a finger to the cross on his chest. "Fish-
hooks for souls," he said. "And we're the fishermen."

Rafe nodded. "Amen."

Joseph held up the sheet of paper, my poor duck feet outlined clearly in black. "I'll be right back," he said. "I need to
cut the soles."

After Joseph disappeared behind the curtain, Rafe bent

down and kissed me. "He and Patty are great," Rafe said, keeping his voice low. "I wouldn't have found Christ without them, but Joseph thinks I'm wrong to want to be a minister with a mainstream Protestant denomination. He thinks it's a waste of time to go to school for eight years before you can preach. I can't make him see that just reading the Bible isn't always enough." Rafe drifted over to look at the purses on the wall. "He says what was good enough for the first Christians should be good enough for the last."

"The last?"

"Oh, you know," Rafe said, "the ones taken up to Heaven in the Rapture before Armageddon comes and the Earth is destroyed."

The Methodist confirmation class I'd taken with Carol hadn't covered the end of the world. "Is this scheduled for sometime soon?"

Rafe shrugged. "Some people think so. It depends on how you read the Book of Revelation. Hey," he said, changing the subject, "did you notice this?" He pointed to a framed certificate hanging above the counter. "It's Joseph's dishonorable discharge. He was in Vietnam, an officer and everything. After he found Christ he wouldn't fight anymore."

The curtain opened and Joseph came back, holding up two brown leather cutouts shaped like my feet. He knelt beside me again, put his hand on my ankle. "Why don't you pop upstairs, Rafe, and say hello to Patience and the kids?" he said. "While we finish the fitting."

"Great idea," Rafe said. "We'd stay longer, but Jesse's dad's in the hospital and she has to get back."

Rafe lifted the curtain and took his turn disappearing. I felt uncomfortable being alone with Joseph, afraid he would ask me if I had found the Lord. He began to measure and then cut leather for the straps. I relaxed. I heard Rafe's voice drifting down from wherever Patience and the kids were—in an upstairs apartment having milk and cookies or an attic sweatshop sewing sandals and welding crosses. Joseph stood up, soles and straps dangling from his hands. "I'm afraid I can't finish them today," he said. "It takes time to stitch them together."

"It must be hard work," I said, standing, too. The floor of the shop felt cold under my bare feet.

"A man has to make a living." He looked around the shop, at the crosses on the counter, at the framed discharge on the wall. Then he turned back to me. "The real work is what's hard," he said. His eyes narrowed, as if taking my measure. I could hear Rafe coming down the stairs and wished he would hurry. "Not everyone is up to that." I could see he didn't think I was. No Patience, he was clearly thinking.

I felt my heart in my chest, beating hard, the way I hoped my father's still was. I imagined his blanketed body lying motionless in the glass cubicle at the hospital. My mother stretched out in her room, lying almost as still. Screw Joseph. "Life is what's hard," I said to him, and I heard my mother's dark tone in my voice. *We're only born to suffer and die.*

Joseph's eyes widened in surprise, as if he'd squeezed my arm and found muscles neither of us knew I had. Rafe stepped out from behind the curtain. "We'd better get a move on or you'll be late," he said.

Joseph nodded. "The sandals will be ready this weekend." I slipped into my flip-flops. Joseph picked my purse up off the floor and handed it to me, his calloused hand briefly touching mine. "I'll pray for your father," he said. "If that's all right with you."

Rafe dropped me at the house. My mother was sitting at the kitchen table, her purse in her lap, ready to go to the hospital. She was trying. But when she began to back our Plymouth out of the garage, her foot slipped off the brake and onto the gas, and we flew backward. The passenger side of the car scraped against the door frame of the garage, metal squealing against metal.

"Damn it," my mother said. She found the brake and hit it hard. We both flew toward the windshield, slamming our foreheads, mine on the dash, hers on the steering wheel. When it was clear we were stopped for good, I unhooked my seat belt and got out to take a look. A long white scratch ran down the side of the blue car. A strip of metal trim hung down, held only by a bit of double-sided tape. I tore the trim loose and tossed it in the garage. It didn't look like anything the car couldn't do without.

"It's okay, Mom," I said, when I got back in. "We can always tell Dad I did it." I was only half joking. I had almost flunked my driver's test trying to parallel park. My mother was still sitting with her forehead resting on the steering wheel. I put my hand on her arm. "Are you okay?" I asked, afraid she was concussed or maybe bleeding.

She raised her head. She was crying, but she looked more angry than sad. "I must have done something terrible in my life to deserve this," she said.

What could she have done? I tried to imagine my mother doing something really wickedly sinful. "Don't say that, Mom," I said. "You didn't do anything to deserve this. Nobody deserves this." *This*. Her life.

"Then there's no point to it," my mother said, "and that's worse."

MY FATHER WAS moved out of intensive care the next day and was released from the hospital a week after that. Carol had gone back to Tallahassee for midterms, so I drove him home. We headed down U.S. 1, me trying to drive as carefully as possible. I was afraid I might hit the brakes and scare my father to death. His lips still looked blue.

"The doctor says I can go back to work next week, if I take it easy," he said to me. "He says I have to do everything I can to avoid stress." My father was still wearing the plastic hospital bracelet with his name on it. He coughed.

"That sounds like a good idea," I said, half listening, half trying to remember the CPR I had learned at camp.

"And Jesse . . ." My father was looking, really looking, at me. It made me nervous. I slowed down.

"Yes, Dad?"

"The doctor said I should think about leaving your mother. He said staying with her, in the current situation—" he paused, picked at the bracelet on his wrist. "He said staying might kill me."

"Oh, Dad," I said. The road blurred. Tears were in my eyes. My father held up his hand.

"I haven't come to any decision. I'm not the kind of man who takes his obligations lightly." My mother, his obligation. He stopped, waiting for me to say something. I didn't want him to die. Not in this car, not ever.

"You do what you have to do, Dad," I said. I knew, sooner or later, what that would be. I tried to imagine the house with just Bertha, Mom, and me. "Carol and I love you, Dad, no matter what."

"Don't miss the turn." My father pointed to the entrance to Indian Heights. I turned, though I wanted to keep driving up U.S. 1 until it ended somewhere in Maine.

Carol called that night. After she talked to Dad, I got on the line.

"I told Dad he should leave while he has the chance," Carol said.

"Hmmm," I said. My mother was in the next room, either watching or sleeping through the news.

"Does that mean you can't talk?" I could hear music from several competing stereos behind Carol and pictured her standing in the hall of her dorm. I couldn't imagine how my sister, who had never been able to read or sleep in the presence of even the slightest noise, could live on a floor with forty girls and as many sets of speakers.

"Hmmm-mmm," I said.

"Are you still seeing Rafe?" Carol said, taking up the slack.

"I guess so." I looked down. I was wearing my new sandals. Rafe had dropped them off that morning, but other than that I had barely seen him. He'd apologized, saying he had to work overtime. I was afraid that just seeing me beside Joseph and Patience had made him change his mind. "We're going out tomorrow night," I said, which was true. I waited for Carol to say something about Rafe, something that would let me know what she thought about him. *He's so great,* or *what a shit.* Instead she changed the subject.

"I've got some big news," she said. "Mac and I are going out." Mac was the lone male in her special education program.

"Wasn't he dating your friend, Nona?" Mac, according to Carol, was always dating one of the girls in the program, each taking a turn as Mac's girl of the month. Now that the girl was her, she'd forgotten her earlier cynicism.

"Don't worry," Carol said. "Nona's still my friend. She understands. We're relaxed about it."

"Well, you certainly sound relaxed."

"Don't let the tone fool you," Carol said, keeping her voice light like she was making a joke. "I'm smoking a lot of pot."

Rafe was late that night. When he arrived, he apologized for the second time that week. He'd had a flat, he said. All the way to and from the movie, he hardly spoke. *This is it,* I was thinking. *He's trying to think of a way to tell me he doesn't want to see me anymore.* As we rattled down U.S. 1, heading for Luna Heights, I consoled myself. Joseph was right. I didn't have what it took to be a minister's wife. I wasn't even sure there was a God.

When we parked in front of the house, Rafe turned to me. "A penny for your thoughts," he said and actually fished in the pockets of his cords and pulled one out. Bright copper, it shone in the light of the nearly full moon.

"You first," I said.

"I was thinking," he said. I winced. I knew what was coming. "I was just thinking," Rafe repeated, "that I love you."

I was amazed. He loved me. I felt a sensation like warm hands cupped around my heart. Rafe had said that's how it felt when Jesus loved you. Maybe Rafe and Christ both loved me. Amazing. Rafe cleared his throat. "Your turn."

"I was thinking that I love you, too." It seemed rude to answer otherwise.

Rafe smiled hugely. "Then I guess we'd better get married."

His logic threw me. I didn't know what to say. I was seventeen. My mother would hate it. My father would hate it. Carol would hate it. When we were little, my mother used to joke that if Carol and I got married before we were twenty-five, she'd write us out of her will. It wasn't a joke, really, except about the inheritance, since there wasn't any money. I looked across the street at my house, darker, if possible, than ever. Carol had left. Soon my father would leave. My mother, well, she was already gone. My life was another NASA disaster. You flip a switch and, *boom,* the mission goes bad. You are just stuck there, the oxygen running lower and lower, the moon and the earth impossibly far away, nothing outside but nothing. Rafe put his arm around my shoulders.

"I guess you're right," I said. "We might as well get married."

Epilogue

One by one, my family left the house in Luna Heights.

Carol graduated and took a job teaching kids with multiple handicaps. She loved her students and they loved her. In the summer, she helped run a camp for them as well.

I married Rafe at a sunrise ceremony in the outdoor amphitheater at my father's junior college. The pictures show Rafe in an embroidered shirt and Joseph's sandals, me in a Mexican wedding dress with a daisy chain in my hair. A friend played "Greensleeves" on the flute.

Bertha, our last surviving pet, came in from a walk one day and fell over, victim of a massive cerebral hemorrhage.

My father moved out of the house. Then he divorced my mother.

But my mother, abandoned by us all, alone in the house in Luna Heights, fought back. Emergencies always brought out the best in her, made her determined and brave. She quit drinking; she quit smoking. She ground up her Valium in the garbage disposal, plastic bottle and all. She went into withdrawal and might have died, but the last thing she did was turn on every light in the house. Mrs. Boggs, noticing how unusual it looked, called the police, who found my mother and called an ambulance.

In the meantime, my father had another heart attack. By then he was living in an apartment, a glorified motel room, and dating a woman who worked at the college. He brought me an amber bracelet from a cruise they took to the Bahamas, but it was too late for him to start again. He had more heart attacks. He stepped down as provost to manage the college's bookstore, but even that was too much for his health. He retired.

By then, I was a Methodist minister's wife. Rafe and I had moved to Tallahassee to go to Florida State University, the school Carol had attended. Though he was only an undergraduate, Rafe was offered a church nearby. North Florida was full of small rural congregations that couldn't afford to pay a minister who'd already gone through seminary. So they made do with retired and student pastors. Our church was about thirty miles south of Tallahassee at a crossroads marked by a blinking yellow warning light. It was the poorest county in Florida, a county without a doctor, a county whose only ambulance belonged to the mortician.

Rafe got two hundred dollars a month, and we got a trailer to live in. It was parked so close to the white frame church I could put my arm out the bedroom window and touch it. One day, when I was helping paint the fellowship hall, I dropped a bucket of paint on my foot and said, "God damn it," loud enough for every member of the congregation to hear. I was still seventeen. I had kids in the youth group I led who were older than I was.

After a year, Rafe had a crisis of faith. He had been having arguments with the minister who was his supervisor, and then that minister, who had problems of his own, went into the pine woods and killed himself with a shotgun. Rafe thought God had stopped loving him. He decided that he shouldn't be a minister. We moved to a big rental house in Tallahassee. Because my father was too ill to live alone, he came to live with us. After spending several months on the psychiatric ward of a VA hospital, my mother moved in, too. Then Rafe decided that God had just been testing him, that he was called to be a minister after all. *God loves me; God loves me not.* The agonies and ecstasies, the ups and downs of it, were too much for me. We got a divorce. My parents, both ill, both living on my father's pension in separate rooms in my rented house, decided to remarry.

Carol and I went with them to the Leon County court house and witnessed their marriage. Then we all went to lunch. My parents bought a double-wide mobile home and spent their days playing Scrabble. They got very good at it. My father knew more large words, but my mother was cleverer at getting triple scores with the simple ones. The games went on for hours and, more often than not, ended in a tie. My mother took my father to the doctor, counted out his pills. She bought new cookbooks and began experimenting, making picture-perfect Shrimp Creole and Chicken Cordon Bleu. Since she'd stopped smoking, she said, everything tasted better.

I helped do the shopping and ran errands for them during the week. Carol, married by then to a fellow special education teacher and living in south Georgia, took care of them on the weekends. My father pretended he wasn't dying, my mother that she didn't live in a trailer. They slept in separate rooms, though sometimes, my mother told me, she would go in and lie down beside my father. He was afraid of dying alone.

The last time my father was in the hospital, I stopped by the trailer to pick up my mother for visiting hours. We were going to take him clean pajamas. He hadn't had a heart attack this time. He was just in to have his medicine adjusted. As we were going out the door, the phone rang. "Hello," my mother answered, then after a pause, asked "Who is this?" But no one was there.

When we got to the hospital, an orderly stopped us in the hall. We would have to wait, he said, the doctor was with my father. He showed us into a small staff conference room with posters on the walls about proper hand-washing procedures. After a few minutes, the doctor came in. My father had had another heart attack, he said. Just a little before, the nurse had been in and saw my father sitting up in bed watching TV. When she came back, my father, who had just turned sixty-five, was dead, the phone in his hand.

"Oh, God," my mother said. If my father had called the trailer, then her last words to her husband had been, *Who is this?*

The young nurse came in, and she had obviously been crying. "He was watching the shuttle launch," she said. "He told me you used to live near Cape Kennedy." She wiped her eyes. "We talked about how beautiful the liftoff was. All that fire."

At my father's funeral, several people went out of their way to tell me how often a widow dies within a year of her husband. Their remarks struck me as both out of place and, in my mother's case, misguided. My parents were not Ozzie and Harriet. My mother did have health problems, especially osteoporosis, her bones thinned to near transparency on the X rays by her years of smoking, drinking, and sleeping. She tucked the sheets in on my father's bed and broke her back. She picked up a can of tomatoes from the pantry and broke it again. She was always breaking bones, but unlike my father's bad heart, it didn't seem like something that killed you. Carol and I thought she'd live for years. We were good daughters. We made plans for taking care of her. We were bad daughters. When we were together, we complained about her bitterly.

But the people at my father's funeral were right. She barely made it a year past his death. She'd sold the trailer and had gone to live with Carol in Georgia. Without my father to take care of, she went back to bed, went back to feeling the black boot over her head. She had nightmares. She told me she dreamed one night that the phone rang, and when she picked it up, it was my father calling. He said, "Why haven't you come to pick me up?"

"Where are you?" my mother asked him, but he wouldn't say. She woke up crying and called the operator, demanding to know which area code my father had been calling from.

One Friday, I was getting ready to drive up for a visit when Carol called. My mother had been rushed to the hospital. She had pneumonia. When I got there, Carol was waiting just outside the swinging double doors of the emergency room. She looked pale and grim. "They had Mom in one of those inflatable shock suits," Carol said. "All she kept saying was, 'Get me out of here.'"

I wondered if Carol remembered saying the same words to me in Cocoa, just before her ambulance ride. This time when the double doors swung open, the doctor came out shaking his head. Get me out of here, my mother had asked, and God or someone answered. She was dead. Like my father, she was barely sixty-five.

WHILE THEY WERE alive, I am sure I was a disappointment to my parents. I married at seventeen and was divorced by twenty. It took me ten years to get my BA. I worked an endless round of minimum wage jobs, delivering phone books, selling shrubberies at a nursery, ringing a bell for the Salvation Army one Christmas when they had run short of bums and believers. I was smart, my mother would have said, but in ways that didn't do me or anybody else much good. After my parents died, all that changed.

I left Florida, went to graduate school, and got a job as a professor. I published two books, a story collection and a novel. As a fiction writer, it amazed me to discover that I could get paid to lie. I remarried and had a daughter. I suppose I finally did what I had dreamed of doing when I left high school. I went far enough and fast enough to become a new and better person. In every way that counts, I have a good and happy life. Often, though, I dream about my parents. Not anything scary or portentous, I just walk into a room and my father and my mother are there, in a house in

Wisconsin they didn't live to see. One night I dreamed my father gave me twenty dollars to take my daughter to see the rerelease of *101 Dalmatians,* a movie he'd taken Carol and me to see. "Get some popcorn," he said. "And keep the change."

IN 1983 CAROL and I went back to Cocoa because she wanted to attend our tenth high school reunion. As only a quasi-member of the Class of '73, I was less keen. I hadn't set foot in Brevard County in eight years. But Carol insisted. "If you're my sister, you'll go," she said on the phone. How could I say no?

At the reunion, I was surprised by how many of the kids we'd grown up with were working at the Cape. After the end of the Apollo program, the Cape, the town, and the county seemed to be closing up shop. Now Mark Lish's little brother, Dana, had the very same job his father had before being laid off.

While we were there, Stephanie (former co-owner of a very well read copy of *Everything You Always Wanted to Know About Sex but Were Afraid to Ask*) offered to take us onto the Kennedy Space Center to see the space shuttle Challenger take off. Stephanie was another second-generation Cape worker and so had passes. This was Challenger's second launch, three years before its disastrous end.

The launch was scheduled for 7:33 in the morning, so we

had to get up before dawn to make it to the Space Center. This was the shuttle with Sally Ride on it. Sally Ride, the first woman astronaut. Sally Ride, whose father had been a teacher at a junior college like my father's. Sally Ride, who, unlike me, had taken science seriously, something that was now about to pay off.

The causeway was crowded with bumper-to-bumper traffic, but we got a good parking spot just opposite Pad 39-A, the old Apollo pad now cut down to fit the shuttle. The boosters on the space shuttles don't make flames like the Saturn Vs did, so we had to be close to get a good view. We sat on the hood of Stephanie's Honda and listened to the countdown on the car radio. Cars and RVs were parked on either side of the causeway for miles. Thousands of people stood in the cool early morning, waiting for the launch, for a second sun to rise. The numbers ticked down: *T minus five, four, three.* The crowd counted along. "Two, one."

White smoke poured out from the pad, the boosters spat flame. The shuttle seemed to hover for a moment before it began to rise, slowly at first, then suddenly racing upward, clearing the tower, heading straight up into the open sky. Above our heads, Challenger banked and turned like the plane it was and headed downrange.

"Ride, Sally, ride," people all around us were chanting. I was yelling, whistling. Carol's voice was hoarse from her allergies, come to visit like ghosts of the past, but she was waving her arms and screaming, too. "Ride, ride."

There will always be disasters, the big black boot waiting to come down on somebody, somewhere, someday. In three years, this same shuttle would explode on takeoff, killing all on board. Cape workers would be laid off again. But that day, for that launch, everything was perfect.

It's important to remember that things can be. I close my eyes and see it: the sun shining the way it can only in the Sunshine State, my sister next to me, both of us shouting with joy because, at long last, an American woman is on her way to space.